What Does the Bible Say About...?

Women and Men

"What Does the Bible Say About...?" Series
Ronald D. Witherup, P.S.S.
Series Editor

Published volumes:

Friendship
Laurie Brink, O.P.

Old Age
Ronald D. Witherup, P.S.S.

Life and Death
John Gillman

Forgiveness
Mary Ann Getty

Angels and Demons
John Gillman and Clifford M. Yeary

Strangers, Migrants, and Refugees
vănThanh Nguy⊠n, S.V.D.

Slavery and Freedom
Catherine Upchurch

Women and Men
John L. Gillman and Florence Morgan Gillman

Inclusion
Donald Senior

Women and Men

John L. Gillman
and
Florence Morgan Gillman

Published by New City Press
202 Comforter Blvd.,
Hyde Park, NY 12538
www.newcitypress.com

Cover design and layout by Miguel Tejerina

Library of Congress Cataloging-in-Publication Data

What Does the Bible Say About Women and Men

Library of Congress Control Number: 2022946257

ISBN: 978-1-56548-716-1 (paper)
ISBN: 978-1-56548-548-8 (e-book)
ISBN: 978-1-56548-697-3 (series ISBN)

Printed in the United States of America

Contents

Series Preface

The Bible remains the world's number one best-seller of all time. Millions of copies in more than two thousand languages and dialects are sold every year, yet how many are opened and read on a regular basis? Despite the impression the Bible's popularity might give, its riches are not easy to mine. Its message is not self-evident and is sometimes hard to relate to our daily lives.

This series addresses the need for a reliable guide to reading the Bible profitably. Each volume is designed to unlock the Bible's mysteries for the interested reader who asks, "What does the Bible say about...?" Each book addresses a timely theme in contemporary culture, based upon questions people are asking today, and explaining how the Bible can speak to these questions as reflected in both Old and New Testaments.

Ideal for individual or group study, each volume consists of short, concise chapters on a biblical theme in non-technical language, and in a style accessible to all. The expert authors have been chosen for their knowledge of the Bible. While taking into account current scholarship, they know how to explain the Bible's teaching in simple language. They are also able to relate the biblical message to the challenges of today's Church and society while avoiding a simplistic use of the biblical text for trying to "prove" a point or defend a position, which is called "prooftexting"—an improper use of the Bible. The focus in these books is on a religious perspective, explaining what the Bible says, or does not say, about each theme. Short discussion questions invite sharing and reflection.

So, take up your Bible with confidence, and with your guide explore "what the Bible says about WOMEN AND MEN."

Introduction

Lake Miramar is a serene destination for many desiring a reprieve from life in the city. From there the distant high-rises of San Diego tower upward in the southeast. The Pacific Ocean unfolds beyond the horizon to the west. The five-mile path around the lake attracts families and friends, coworkers and couples, those seeking a solitary space. This is one of our favorite places. About every week, we load bikes on our refurbished Ford F-150 and take a ride around these peaceful waters. Afterward we relax at a picnic table, watching a few geese ambling around, ducks paddling through the gentle ripples, an occasional boat passing by. Enjoying the gentle breeze, we take time to have some relaxed conversations. In this book, we want to share with you, individually and together as a couple, our reflections, many of which we pondered in that peaceful setting.

The Bible has much to say about men and women. Let's start with the high praise the psalmist proclaims before God: "You have made them [women and men] a little lower than God, / and crowned them with glory and honor" (Psalm 8:5). The biblical stories feature notable female figures such as matriarchs and queens, prophetesses and an apostle, missionaries and a deacon. Among them are Rebekah and Rachel, Bathsheba and Jezebel, Miriam and Mary the mother of Jesus, Hannah and Elizabeth, Junia and Phoebe. Similarly, on the male side there are patriarchs and kings, lawgivers and prophets, evangelists and coworkers. They include Abraham and Isaac, Moses and David, Isaiah and Luke, Paul and Timothy, and of course that Galilean peasant, Jesus. Among the couples we encounter Queen Esther and King Ahasuerus, Hosea and Gomer, Prisca and Aquila. As moral agents, each of these people, and many others we will meet, are capable of admirable as well as less exemplary behaviors. Each in his or her own manner gives expression to a form of culturally shaped masculinity or femininity.

Some of these are among the heroes and heroines whom many admire. None of them, however, is without a shadow side. Even Jesus himself is recorded as making what seem to be insensitive comments to his mother and other women. Especially pronounced are the shortcomings of figures like Queen Jezebel or the great King David, who took Bathsheba as his eighth wife after scheming to have her husband Uriah killed in battle. On the other hand, the goodness of Job and Ruth, of Jesus and Mary, is hardly up for debate.

In recent decades, prompted in part by the rise of the feminist movement, there have been a boatload of studies about biblical women and men. Drawing upon insights from these analyses, we will dialogue with such contemporary themes as gender identity and the complexity of male and female relationships. Our hope is that such exploration will assist you in becoming more attuned to your own self-understanding as an embodied sexual person, including the way you express your femininity or masculinity.

Androcentrism: He Held the Pen!

Before we go further, let's look at the broad landscape. First, keep in mind that the Bible, the inspired Word of God, was written by human authors and, as far as the evidence indicates, all men—probably urban elites—who were writing primarily for other men. (Thus, the expression *androcentrism*, from Greek meaning "male-centered.") As might be expected, the human authors shaped the material in ways that reflected their predominant cultural perspectives. Men decided, whether intentionally or not, how to tell the stories and whom to include. The effect was to enshrine the male point of view as normative. Incidentally, named women comprise no more than eight percent of all named biblical people. Lost to us are the host of female leaders and prophets, innumerable wives and daughters, whose lives contributed to the total fabric of the biblical people of God. It is not surprising then that male characters and concerns overshadow the more limited attention given to females and their concerns. The task for the attentive reader is to read the biblical text closely as it has been passed down in order to uncover feminine perspectives as much as possible.

The male bias in Scripture is reflected in the naming and the numbers. The first five books of the Bible, called the Torah or Pentateuch, are traditionally known as the five books of Moses, although most scholars believe they were written only in his name. Other documents named for men include the 150 Psalms of David, the two books of Samuel, and the two books of Kings. Joshua and Job each have a book named after them, as do sixteen male prophets. Only three books, Ruth, Esther, and Judith, are named after women.

Back to the numbers: we hear about the twelve sons of Jacob and the twelve apostles (all male), who also have a book named after them—the Acts of the Apostles. When it comes to numbers, women are not placed in the most positive light. We read, for example, that Mary Magdalene had had seven demons (Luke 8:2), and the Samaritan woman had five husbands (John 4:18).

We will begin our discussion of women and men by looking at the two Creation accounts in Genesis and the famous Pauline text in Galatians 3:28, and then consider several men and women who appear throughout the Bible. Along the way we invite you to reflect on how much your lives have been sustained by ordinary men and women whom you have encountered.

The scope of our project limits what we can cover. One topic we will have to put aside is the use of male and female imagery in the Bible to portray God, who, as pure spirit, is neither, transcending sex and gender. As we move into the eight chapters of this book we invite you to draw upon your own experience, to engage the questions for reflection, and to be attentive to the promptings of the Holy Spirit.

Chapter One

Gender and Sexual Identity in the Postmodern Age

The effort to understand and integrate our identity as flesh-and-blood human beings involves coming to grips with our bodies, which are either male or female. This is, of course, based on the traditional belief that gender can be divided into two parts, male and female—a concept that some call the gender binary—and that gender, our lived expression or experience of our sex, a primarily biological concept, is an absolute and rigidly defined part of our identity. This would be the standard view expressed in the Bible and characteristic of Western history. Those who think that gender should not be a binary refer to people who "identify with" their biological sex as cisgender, or simply "cis." Others, referred to as transgender, or simply "trans," feel strongly that their gender identity does not match their biological sex. Still others do not understand themselves exclusively as either male or female but rather as nonbinary. Among the 1.2 million people who identify as nonbinary in the United States are those who variously refer to themselves as queer, bisexual, pansexual, or asexual.[1] At this point readers who grew up, as we did, with a traditional understanding that a human person is either male or female as indicated by one's biological sex may find their heads spinning. This is equally true of the biblical perspective, which stems from a pre-scientific world view in which these categories did not even exist. This does not mean, however, that the Bible does not speak to these issues. On the contrary, if one reads and interprets carefully, basic principles about human existence, such as the Bible's overall emphasis on human dignity, this can inform our modern understanding which impacts how women and men interact.

In recent decades gender identity has become a much-debated "hot topic." It is beyond the scope of this brief book to enter this discussion except to note how such seminal texts as Genesis 1:27–28 and Galatians 3:28 have been brought to it. The crucial issue of gender identity, which affects the lives of many, ranging from individuals to their families to society at large, is currently much discussed by both science and theology. Faith groups have weighed in, some taking strong positions on questions such as the understanding of how the roles of men and women are shaped by sex.

Increasing Recognition of Women (But Not Enough)

Writing this first chapter in the middle of Women's History Month (March 2021), we are aware of the growing number of news items, books, and films that feature women in key leadership roles. Regarding the Christian tradition, after highlighting the role of women who distinguished themselves, including Euodia and Syntyche (Philippians

4:2), Pope Benedict XVI in 2007 made the statement that "without the generous contribution of many women, the history of Christianity would have developed very differently."[2]

That is true as well of world history. To cite just a few more recent women who have made a difference, we note the remarkable story of Malala Yousafzai, a Nobel Peace Prize recipient (2014), who as a Pakistani teenager faced intense opposition from the Taliban as she stood up for female education. Another is the Australian feminist Helen Reddy, whose iconic song "I Am Woman" was named by the UN as the theme for the 1975 "Year of the Woman" and prominently featured for International Women's Day in 2021. The poet Maya Angelou, through her poetry and public speaking, inspired women to overcome sex discrimination. She was awarded the 2010 Presidential Medal of Freedom.

Not to be overlooked is the #MeToo movement—first appearing in social media in 2006—which unleashed the power of stories by women whose voices have often remained silent: women who have been sexually harassed, assaulted, and abused. This movement spread rapidly and empowered women to speak out against sexual abuse and harassment across the spectrum from the workplace to politics. While there is nothing comparable to this movement in the biblical tradition, stories of sexual abuse, such as the rape of Dinah by Shechem and the rape of Tamar by Amnon (Genesis chapter 34; 2 Samuel chapter 13), could spark such a movement. In a fictional account of a biblical text (*The Red Tent*, 1997), Anita Diamant beautifully imagines the world of Dinah, where the women of the family use their time in the red tent to tell their stories. This is a place where they felt empowered to share their experiences.

What Does It Take to Be a Real Man?

Like women, men too have figured prominently in the media as well as national events and organizations. International Men's Day (November 19), first observed in 1992, focuses on "improving gender relations, highlighting male role models, and promoting positive expressions of masculinity." One of the largest gatherings was the Million Man March (October 16, 1995) organized for black men on the themes of atonement, reconciliation, and personal responsibility.

There has been no lack of movies in which men dominate those around them (such as *The Godfather*, 1972) and embody an alpha male persona (*Unforgiven*, 2013). Other films project a different way of being masculine, such as *Unbroken* (2014), based on Laura Hillenbrand's best-selling book by the same title (2010), which features the perseverance and spiritual transformation of Louis Zamperini, an Olympic track star and World War II prisoner of war. He returned to Japan to forgive his captors. *John, who once having had the honor of sharing a quiet lunch with Louis, is inspired, as are so many, by his inner strength and resilience.*

Like the popular view of femininity, what we usually think of as masculinity is to a great extent a culturally shaped way of expressing one's manhood. Women, for example, in some societies have been socialized to be gentle, passive, vulnerable, and deferential. Men, on the other hand, are expected to be leaders, powerful, risk-takers, in control, and authoritative. In recent years research into masculinity has explored the pressures men experience to become "real men" by conforming to cultural expectations. Their behavior in response to these pressures is typically to manifest competitiveness, risk-taking, control, strength, and even aggression, and above all to have nothing to do with manifestations of femininity.

The anxiety and fear of not living up to these expectations can lead to what is sometimes called fragile masculinity, where men react strongly and usually aggressively to any perception of femininity, in other words, weakness, in their behavior. Cultural expectations that socialize men to be aggressive (interpersonally and particularly romantically), to look down on women, and to avoid expressing emotions and vulnerability in healthy ways are sometimes referred to as toxic masculinity.

Efforts to assist men in reclaiming more authentic expressions of being masculine include participation in groups like *Men as Learners and Elders* (M.A.L.E.), founded by Fr. Richard Rohr. *Illuman* (neologism for "illumination" and "human") is a similar group that uses ritual, teaching, and communication strategies to assist men who are seeking a life-changing spirituality. This reminds us of how Mark, early in his Gospel, reports that Jesus called the apostles to "come away to a deserted place all by yourselves and rest awhile" (6:31). We might wonder how they reflected on their radically changed selves through the encounter with the carpenter from Nazareth.

As we shall see, a biblical view of sexuality and gender is more about embracing true human existence that goes beyond culturally defined stereotypes.

For Reflection:

- How do you understand the issues of gender identity facing the modern world today? How would you assess the relationships between men and women today?
- What can a faith perspective based on the Bible bring to contemporary issues of sex and gender?

Chapter Two

Men and Women Enter Stage Center

The relationship between a person's biological sex and gender identity has received no lack of attention from church, science, and society at large in recent years. The long-standing tradition holds firmly to what is called the male/female sexual binary. This means that there are only two sexes, the male and the female. Besides scientific and our own personal observation of the existence of the sexes, a biological fact of life we all learn from our earliest years, Genesis 1:27 is often cited as the scriptural basis mirroring such a conviction. If that is the case then what about those who are transgender, a term referring to persons who sense that their gender identity is different from that assigned at birth due to their female or male anatomy? By contrast, those whose gender identity corresponds to their biological sex at birth—and this is the vast majority of the population—are cisgender. There is also a very small percentage of people who are intersex, that is, born with ambiguous genitalia, but who are otherwise (e.g., on the chromosomal level) female or male. While the Bible does not directly address such issues, one thing that is clear is the need to respect women and men equally in their essential *human* dignity. Personhood extends beyond one's psychosexual identity to embrace the full human experience.

The Vatican document "'Male and Female He Created Them': Towards a Path of Dialogue on the Question of Gender Theory in Education" (June 2019), upholds the male/female binary perspective, based on the belief that gender concerns how the "sexual difference between men and women is lived out in a variety of cultures."[3] This instruction also mentions several times the importance of listening to the experience of the other. This openness to dialogue is more critical than ever. A 2019 study found that "thirty-five percent of transgender teens reported that they had attempted suicide in the past year."[4] Dialogue between theologians and social scientists may be particularly fruitful in sorting out the issues pertaining to biological sex and gender identity.

With this brief overview of very complex issues, let us approach the biblical tradition asking what it means for all human beings, however we feel about our bodies, to be created in the image and likeness of God.

In the Beginning

After five momentous biblical days, symbolizing the over thirteen billion years during which our universe is estimated to have taken shape, with the lighting in place and a supporting cast of living creatures at the ready, the divine director is set for the big reveal on day six. Not unlike expectant couples who plan festive gatherings to reveal the sex of their unborn child, God's creative word makes known the stars of the show. On day six of the first

Creation account in Genesis, the script sets the scene for an event unlike any other: "Then God said, 'Let us make humankind in our image, according to our likeness'" (1:26a; see also 1:27a).

Whereas the gods in much ancient mythology related to humans—typically presented as descendants of the gods—as little more than playthings at the mercy of the gods' fickle machinations, the God of the Bible chose to fashion humans as the pinnacle of all creation. Apart from all other forms of nature which are indeed "charged with the grandeur of God," as the Jesuit poet Gerard Manley Hopkins so famously expressed it, the Holy One "crowned [human beings] with glory and honor" (Psalm 8:5).

There are several features of God's desire to create humankind that merit further exploration. Perhaps you have noticed that the narrator speaks of the divine with the plural "us" and "our." Doesn't this clash with the firm Judeo-Christian conviction that God is one (Deuteronomy 6:4; 1 Corinthians 8:6)? The Hebrew word used for the divine name is *Elohim*, which literally means "Gods." What's going on here? In a few places in the Old Testament, God is presented as having a council of supernatural beings sometimes referred as the "host of heaven" whom God consults (1 Kings 22:19–22). This suggests that the choice to share divine life with humankind is a well-thought-out decision arrived at with the heavenly host, although the first couple ran treacherously off the rails from how God intended humans to act (Genesis chapters 2—3).

Next, observe that the author calls God's creation "humankind"—'male' and 'female' do not enter the scene until the end of verse 27—a word that translates the Hebrew *adam*, a singular noun referring to humanity as a whole, its dominant meaning in the Old Testament, but which later becomes the proper name Adam. The point not to be missed is that the creation of our common humanity precedes the specification about the division into biological sex. This point is significant regarding the issues mentioned above. The next verse does articulate the standard biblical viewpoint of the binary nature of sex. Regarding those who are transgender, the Vatican document cited above rejects the stance that there is some "liquidity" and "fluidity" regarding sexual identity apart from gender binary as being "nothing more than a confused concept of freedom in the realm of feelings and wants."[5] Nevertheless this issue continues to be passionately debated in both church and society.

Living Icons

The use of *adam* in 1:26 opens the way for a clever pun in the second Creation account (Genesis 2:4–25) where *adam*, understood in this context as an individual, is fashioned out of *adamah* ("the dust of the ground," 2:7). In English we could express this close connection between the human being and the dust, or soil, as *human* and *humus* (the organic component of soil). *Adam* is also related to *adom* (25:30), meaning "red," the color of *dom* (9:5), meaning "lifeblood." In a culture too often characterized by an "us" versus "them" mentality, we must remember that we all bleed the same color, and from a genetic perspective we share DNA that is 99.9 percent identical to that of all humans.[6] As divinely shaped *adam*-creatures, all of us together form one human community whose richly variegated characteristics, from skin tones to personalities, reflect the splendor of God's evolving creation.

How awesome that humankind is fashioned in the divine image (Greek, *eikōn*; 1:26, 27; 9:6), each person representing a living icon of the invisible God. Many churches in Orthodox Christian traditions have an iconostasis with images of the saints, an elaborate screen that separates the altar from the main section of the church where the faithful gather. Let's imagine for a moment the human community as a continuous vibrant iconostasis spanning the globe reflecting the divine.

This symbolic relationship between humanity and the Deity is sometimes referred to with the Latin expression *imago Dei* (image of God; see Genesis 5:1). Each person is an *imago Dei* at the core of one's existence throughout one's lifespan from before birth (Jeremiah 1:5) to the last breath. The *imago Dei* is a divine characteristic that remains integral to the person, even though it may be tarnished by misdeeds. Thus, from the beginning God is intimately involved in the human enterprise, and being created in the image of God creates in us the capacity for union with God. We originate from God and our destiny is to be reunited fully with God.

Having named the creation of humankind, the author of Genesis moves from the generic singular *adam* in 1:27a to the plural in 1:27b: "in the image of God he created them; / male and female he created them." In this verse male and female are biological designations; both are blessed by God and both have the capacity for fertility as indicated by the divine command: "Be fruitful and multiply" (1:28). The writer clearly names the two sexes as equals; each reflects the image of God. Martin Luther King, Jr., poignantly makes this point: "We must never forget [that] . . . there are no gradations in the image of God. Every man [generic] from a treble white to a bass black is significant on God's keyboard."[7]

In the first Creation account there is no hint that the man was created before the woman; they are co-created by and instructed to be co-creators with God. Note that men do not have priority, authority, or dominance over women. From the beginning a balance between men and women is established, but after this event, many accounts in the subsequent biblical narrative and throughout the course of history up to the present tell a different story. Few would argue with Pope Francis's assessment in the encyclical letter *Fratelli Tutti* (2020) that society "is still far from reflecting clearly that women possess the same dignity and identical rights as men," adding that "it is unacceptable that some have fewer rights by virtue of being women."[8] He points out the deplorable perpetuation of slavery, when human persons created in the image and likeness of God, "whether by coercion, or deception, or by physical or psychological duress . . . are deprived of their freedom, sold and reduced to being the property of others."[9] Speaking in the spirit of a prophet, Mother Teresa remarked: "If everyone could see the image of God in his neighbor, do you think we would still need tanks and generals?"[10]

In his teaching on marriage and divorce, Jesus quotes Genesis 1:27b: "But from the beginning of creation, 'God made them male and female'" (Mark 10:6), to support his conclusion: "Therefore what God has joined together, let no one separate" (10:9). The corresponding passage in Matthew also includes this verse from Genesis, but in his Gospel Jesus further notes that "Moses allowed you to divorce your wives," although "from the beginning it was not so" (Matthew 19:8, see 19:1–12).

The Divine Response to Loneliness

The second Creation account offers a different perspective from the first; there is a shift from equality in the relationship between male and female in Genesis chapter 1 to a worldview in Genesis chapter 2 where the culturally influenced biblical writer presents women as secondary to men. Even within that perspective, however, the theme of a complementary partnership between man and woman is expressed. The first account, emphasizing equality, is more about biology (the generative); the second is more about anthropology (the nature of humanity), built on an assumption about hierarchy, yet also including the relational nature of humans.

In the second account, God forms the man from the dust of the ground (2:7; see 1 Timothy 2:13), then the woman from one of the man's ribs (2:21–22). According to one commentator, this description is not about biology but rather lineage, as indicated by the biblical genealogies where the initiator is male. This is the case both for Adam and his descendants (Genesis chapter 5), and the ancestors of Jesus, who are traced back to Abraham (Matthew 1:1–17) and Adam (Luke 3:23–38). The ordering of creation in Genesis chapter 2 is utilized by Paul in declaring that "man was not made from woman, but woman from man" when he argues for proper dress at public prayer. In this same passage Paul underscores the interdependence of men and women: "Indeed, man was not made from woman, but woman from man" and "...in the Lord woman is not independent of man or man independent of woman" (1 Cor 1:8, 11). Later, either Paul or someone writing in his name says: "For Adam was formed first, then Eve; and Adam was not deceived, but the woman was deceived..." (1 Timothy 2:13–14). Unfortunately, these passages, along with others, have been enlisted by church and society at various periods in history to maintain the subordination of women.

What gets overlooked when such an agenda is pressed, however, is the divine awareness in Genesis chapter 2 of the human condition. God, for whom creation is a work in progress, observes that "It is not good that the man [*adam*] should be alone," and so seeks a remedy: "I will make him a helper as his partner" (2:18). The Hebrew expression for "helper as his partner" literally means "a helper, someone who stands over against," meaning to have one's separate identity. This does not indicate a person who is inferior, but rather a counterpart, an equal, who is a remedy for human loneliness. Whether in marriage or in close friendships, the other is a valuable partner offering support during troubling times like sickness and the loss of employment, or providing challenge when one's behavior is disturbing or decision making is unsound.

In the divine perspective, then, humans are made for relationship, for partnership, not isolation. This applies to both the man and the woman in this narrative (the term *marriage* is not used in this passage), and on a broad scale, to all men and women who at the very core of their identity are relational by nature, drawn to form bonds of connection.

This theme of human encounter is well articulated by the Jewish scholar Martin Buber's famous work, *I and Thou* (1923), a reflection on relational participation with the other. The "I-Thou" interaction is characterized by reciprocity and mutuality. On the opposite side of the spectrum are "I-It" transactions (impersonal); though necessary and useful at times—for example, interacting with a cashier—these pose a risk by neither recognizing nor respecting the *imago Dei* of the other. With reference to women who are so treated, the #MeToo movement and other feminist and social justice efforts are a poignant and vigorous response. These efforts give voice to women and girls who are victims of violence and abuse, humiliation and exploitation, and to those who are constrained by poverty and deprived of fundamental rights. Such situations rob them of their dignity as human beings made in the image of God.

Trouble in Paradise

Despite the strong bond Adam and Eve enjoyed with each other, neither fared well in the Garden of Eden (Genesis chapter 3), as we see in a story that comes right on the heels of the two Creation accounts. Both the man and woman are commanded not to eat from the tree in the middle of the garden. While the man remains silent, the woman acts, in part, out of her desire for wisdom (3:6). Although God warned both not to eat from that tree (2:17; 3:3), first the woman and then the man did so, thus disobeying the divine command (3:6).

Then the blame game begins. Unfortunately, the blessed partnership between the sexes acclaimed in chapter 2 quickly deteriorates into opposition and conflict. In a vigorous denial of responsibility, the man puts the onus on both the woman and God (3:12). In the acerbic and witty early feminist commentary, *The Woman's Bible* (1898), Elizabeth Cady Stanton adds a flair of drama quoting Adam's protest before God: "'The woman thou gavest to be with me, she gave me and I did eat,' he whines—trying to shield himself at his wife's expense!" Stanton then expresses her amazement "that upon such a story men have built up a theory of their superiority!"[11] But Adam's complaint gets him nowhere; nothing in the unfolding narrative absolves him of his complicity. Unfortunately, the blessed partnership between the genders acclaimed in Genesis 2 quickly deteriorates into opposition and conflict in Genesis 3. How agonizing it becomes when relationships that begin with intimacy and affection wither, and, left unattended, die on the vine, leaving a residue of painful memories.

God then imposes penalties on all three involved: the serpent, Eve, and Adam. All are culpable, yet in the history of interpretation most of the blame has been heaped on the woman. To his credit, the man appropriately names his wife Eve (resembling the word for "living") "because she was the mother of all living" (3:20).

To What Extent Is There Gender Equity?

We now transition from our discussion of equality between the sexes (first Creation account, Genesis chapter 1), the relational nature of man and woman (second Creation account, Genesis chapter 2), and the aftermath (the Fall, Genesis chapter 3), to one of the most frequently cited texts about the relationship among races, social classes, and sexes in the New Testament. In his feisty, tendentious letter to the Galatians, Paul writes: "There is no longer Jew or Greek, there is no longer slave or free, there is no longer male and female; for all of you are one in Christ Jesus" (3:28).

This bold declaration is often cited as an emancipatory text for sex equality within society and the church, including leadership positions. The distance to gender parity (with respect to the categories of economics, education, health, and political empowerment) in North America is 76% (2021 study). The gender pay gap is only slightly better. According to the U.S. Bureau of Statistics, in 2020 women earned 82 cents to the dollar earned by men.[12] Paid lay ministers in the Catholic Church (most of whom are women) earn 76 cents for every dollar earned by male clergy (2014 study).[13] In fact, most of ministry is actually done by unpaid laity, primarily women. Pope Francis has called this disparity "pure scandal."[14] In 2021 he increased leadership roles for women in the Vatican. A 2019 study showed that in broader society women score better than men on several key leadership qualities.[15]

Discussion of this passage sometimes gives rise to questions about ordination of women in the church. However, in its *original context* there is no certainty Paul was referring to the ordination of any person since ordination *as understood today* was not a concept Paul used. In that regard, the Congregation for the Doctrine of the Faith argued that "this passage does not concern ministries: it only affirms the universal calling to divine filiation, which is the same for all."[16] Let's take a closer look. In Galatians 3:28 Paul highlights three polarities, namely, ethnicity, social status, and sex, respectively, leading up to an emphatic conclusion that in Christ, all are one. This formal principle means that one ethnicity is not privileged over another, the free are not privileged over the enslaved, and males are not privileged over females. Thus, situated in its immediate literary context (3:23–29), this passage is about the believers' faith in Christ, which links them to Abraham, known for his faith. Secondly, all, without distinction, are children of

God, meaning they have been adopted by God and are full heirs of God; indeed they are co-heirs with Christ (Romans 8:17). This adoption comes through baptism into Christ, symbolized by the clothing metaphor of having put on Christ. The passage is more about baptismal identity than anything else.

Let's Ask Paul

One of the first interpretive principles that Pauline scholars learn is to explain Paul by Paul, using his literary correspondence to elucidate such challenging passages as Galatians 3:28. We invite you to join us in an imaginative conversation with Paul about this intriguing verse.

> *John*: Paul, your expression "there is no longer male and female" raises some questions. Could you help us understand what you mean?
>
> *Paul*: Remember, I was fired up when I wrote to the Galatians. I almost lost it when I called them foolish and bewitched (3:1), since they believed in another gospel contrary to what I proclaimed to them (1:6–8). By saying "male and female" I was referring to the Creation story in Genesis 1:27. My point was to challenge men and women to take a hard look at how their attitudes, behaviors, and practices toward each other reflect

their status as baptized people in Christ, as one in Christ, indeed as a new creation (6:15).

Florence: Yes, what caught my attention was your reference to baptism in verse 27. Some years ago I wrote my doctoral thesis on the first part of Romans 6:5: "For if we have been united with him in a death like his . . .", exploring how radically transforming baptism is for a Christian. In your patriarchal society, however, which also characterizes much of our world today, were some of the baptized—for example, men like you and Peter—nevertheless more privileged than others?

Paul: Wow! That is a tough subject. As you know, in my letter to the Galatians I relate how I confronted Peter because he yielded to pressures from the circumcision party and stopped eating with the Gentiles. That is why I wrote "no longer Jew or Greek" (standing for all Gentiles). Now, about relations between the sexes, I confess that I have not been consistent culturally (see 1 Corinthians 11:2–16) and have not always followed through on the core conviction I expressed in 3:28. Among my most trusted coworkers and leaders in the early communities of believers in Christ were women like the deacon Phoebe, the apostle Junia, and Lydia, the head of her household who hosted gatherings of believers. By the way, I'm not surprised by your questions. I've read your book about the women I knew, including some of my wonderful collaborators![17]

John: Going back to the question of baptism, years ago I attended a seminar given by the Benedictine liturgist Aidan Kavanagh, who noted that in the early church all the baptized became *christoi*, a people who were anointed, like the "*Christos*-messiah," as priests and kings.[18] Is this emphasis on embodying Christ through an anointing received by newly baptized women and men consistent with your own view?

Paul: Very much so. In another letter I clearly affirm that God in Christ "has anointed us, by putting his seal on us and giving us his Spirit in our hearts" (2 Corinthians 1:21–22).

Florence: Paul, I sometimes think many members of today's church do not realize how profoundly baptism should affect our identities and daily lives. Have we lost something?

Paul: I think your observation reflects an area of renewal that the church is working on, but perhaps not widely enough. To really understand the transformation baptism offers to a person is to come to a very deep, life-changing realization. I think there are many Christians in your era who don't give much thought to their baptisms (maybe because they were infants!). You may need to much more fully explore the profound thoughts behind what I was expressing to the Galatians. I recommend you reclaim your baptismal identity in Christ.

John and Florence: Thanks Paul! Galatians 3:28 continues to challenge us as Christians today to seriously take on and implement your vision.

For Reflection:

- How do you understand the relationship between biological sex and gender expression? To what extent do the Creation narratives influence your perspective?
- How do you hear in your own life Paul's baptismal affirmation that "there is no longer male and female; for all of you are one in Christ Jesus"?

Chapter Three

Her Surprise and His Response

On one level the counterparts to Adam and Eve in the Old Testament are Joseph and Mary in the New Testament. Instead of enjoying the delights of Paradise, the first couple ate the forbidden fruit in the desire to attain a quality reserved to the Divine, and they paid the price. The woman and then the man yielded to the temptation put before them and they lost their innocence. Growing up in humble places, Mary and Joseph, another woman and man, each faced a perplexing dilemma and responded with trust and courage. Because of her role Mary has been named the second Eve,[19] and Joseph is securely placed in the family tree of Adam (Luke 3:23–38). Their significance, of course, is intimately related to the life and mission of their firstborn son.

Devotional practices centered on this couple, especially Mary, have been growing since the days of the early church, and have taken an important place in many people's experience of Christian spirituality. Shrines grow up to honor them, patronages are assigned to them, and innumerable churches are named after them.

John's origin has something to do with the latter. He recalls his father, with a gleam in his eye, pointing out the parish hall of St. Mary's Church in a small village in southern Indiana where he met his future wife, John's mother.

John took Joseph as his Confirmation name. Like Saint Joseph, John's father and some of his ancestors from Germany were carpenters, a trade that John also learned in his youth from his father and his brothers. At home as a youngster, John's family regularly said the rosary, a practice that is still one of his own, though less often now.

Joseph was declared by successive popes the patron of the universal church, the patron of workers, and the patron of a happy death. Mary has been named the patroness of the United States under her title Our Lady of the Immaculate Conception.

Mary and Joseph have both been declared saints of the church. They are honored through several feasts in the liturgical calendar; their image is represented on sacred icons from the Orthodox tradition and their bodily form is sculptured, carved, or cast in statues in the Western Church. Except for some icons and the feast of the Holy Family, they are often portrayed individually. The parish churches that John and Florence attended in their youth both had a statue of Mary in the left transept, and one of Joseph in the right transept. This may have created a misperception that de-emphasized their marriage, despite the fact that there is a memorial to Joseph, the Husband of Mary.

Intended to honor Mary the mother and Joseph the legal father of the Savior, devotional practices sometimes obscured or even distorted the ordinary humanity of this couple whose lives were rooted in a first-century cultural, political, and religious context marked by turbulence and insecurity. Almost forgetting her powerful, prophetic voice in the Magnificat (Luke 1:46–55), popular devotions sometimes portrayed Mary as meek and mild, a compliant and docile servant, humble and passive, sweet and submissive.

Ron Rolheiser, a well-known religious author, has remarked that "the Mary of Devotions is often so enshrined in piety, over-simplicity, and asexuality" as if to protect her "from human complexity."[20] At the other end of the spectrum she has been raised high on a pedestal approaching the status of a goddess; some even refer to her as "co-redemptrix," a theological suggestion which Pope Francis has repeatedly warned is inaccurate.[21] We invite you to journey with us as we explore some of what is known about Mary and Joseph in their everyday lives.

Mary and Joseph at Ground Level

With fresh eyes let us turn to the witness of Scripture and insights from archaeology to glean what can be learned about Mary and Joseph. Most of what we know about them is contained in the infancy narratives related in the first few chapters of Matthew's and Luke's Gospels. Joseph plays the primary role in the former and Mary the more prominent role in the latter. Both evangelists structure the genealogy of Joseph from a patrilineal perspective, men begetting men, traced back to Abraham by Matthew and to Adam by Luke. Women are excluded except for the four reported in Matthew. These are Tamar, who pretended to be a prostitute; Rahab, a prostitute; Ruth, a widow initiating a sexual encounter; and Bathsheba, a woman taken in adultery (see chapter 4 of this book for more about these women). The shocking circumstances of these unlikely heroines, who are nevertheless ancestors of the Davidic line, point to the extramarital pregnancy of Mary, the young peasant woman from Galilee. Mary's pregnancy becomes the catalyst for the infancy narratives. In this chapter our intention is to discuss Mary and Joseph together, thus honoring their relationship as husband and wife and parents of their firstborn child, Jesus.

Mary and Joseph were both from insignificant hamlets with a population around 400. Joseph was probably from Bethlehem in Judea, where, in compliance with the tax-related census ordered by Caesar Augustus, he took Mary and their child (Luke 2:1–5). And Mary, whose Hebrew name would have been Miriam, was from Nazareth (Luke 1:26), a few miles south of Sepphoris, the thriving administrative center of Galilee where much building was taking place in this era. Nazareth held no claim to fame, as indicated in Nathanael's cynical question to Philip, "Can anything good come out of Nazareth?" (John 1:46). Life for a Jewish peasant girl like Mary would have been bound up with relative poverty and hard work. The Gospels give no indication how Joseph and Mary, coming from places far apart, actually met.

The first time Joseph is mentioned, he is identified as the husband of Mary (Matthew 1:16), a relationship that is referenced several more times in the Gospels. By trade Joseph was a *tekton*, a Greek term usually translated as "carpenter" (Matthew 13:55; Mark 6:3), but which generally referred to any craftsman who worked with his hands. When he lived in Nazareth, where the resources were rock rather than wood, archaeologists suggest that Joseph probably worked as a stone mason, maybe in Sepphoris. According to custom he would have taught his son Jesus the trade; perhaps the two of them made daily trips to the work sites at Sepphoris.

At a young age, about 14 for Mary and 16 for Joseph (the apocryphal gospel the *Protoevangelium of James*, however, says that Joseph was an old man at the time), typical for the culture of the time, they were betrothed to one another. This meant they were truly husband and wife although they were not yet living together. Breaking a betrothal was equivalent to divorce. We don't know further details of Mary and Joseph's betrothal, but typically marriages at the time were arranged by the fathers of the man and woman, although it could also have been negotiated between Joseph himself and Mary's father.

Response to Pregnancy

When Joseph became aware of Mary's pregnancy (Matthew 1:18), he must have been deeply troubled, suspecting that his betrothed had been unfaithful. His initial response was to divorce her quietly, and thus not expose her to public shame. As a betrothed woman not yet living with her future husband Mary, and thus Joseph, were both dealing with an unintended pregnancy. They may have been faced with a range of emotions from shock to guilt, perhaps even joy. For such a couple today, then come momentous decisions: to have the unborn come to full term or to have an abortion? If the former, to keep the infant or put the baby up for adoption. A growing number of unmarried couples and single women decide to have children, and this choice presents its own challenges. According to one study, young women from 18–24 have "the highest rate of unintended pregnancy" and among this group, "around 60% of unintended pregnancies result in childbirth, 40% in abortion, and less than 2% in adoption."[22] Similar to Joseph, men today may respond to the news of unmarried pregnancy with perplexity, even fright. Some, although not all, live up to their responsibility and remain involved to support the woman they impregnated.

While the response of the Catholic Church to single mothers has vastly improved in recent decades, pastoral practices regarding baptism, for example, vary widely from parish to parish. Pope Francis has called the denial of baptism for babies from single mothers "pastoral cruelty."[23] In 2013 he reached out to a single mother and offered to baptize her child. Another harsh practice has been the firing of single female employees of Catholic institutions for becoming pregnant. The fathers involved have rarely been known to incur the same penalty.

The Dreams of a Righteous Man

Like Tamar in Genesis (38:26) and Zechariah and Elizabeth in Luke (1:6), Joseph is among the few in the Bible who have been called upright or "righteous" (Matthew 1:19), because of his obedience to the Law. Although he could have had Mary stoned, he chose to be merciful by refusing "to expose her to public disgrace," instead planning "to dismiss her quietly" (Matthew 1:19; see Deuteronomy 22:20–22).

That's when an angel got into the act, appearing to Joseph in a dream and informing him that Mary's child was conceived by the Holy Spirit (Matthew 1:20). By accepting the child as his own and naming him, Joseph places this child in the dynasty of David. Joseph and Mary, in renewing their socially unusual commitment to each other, "provide an example of the frequently countercultural and contested discipleship Jesus will require of his disciples."[24]

In obedience to a second dream, Joseph took the child and his nursing wife to Egypt to escape the despotic reach of murderous Herod. There they dwelt as foreigners, until returning after Herod's death to Judea, presumably Bethlehem, as prompted by Joseph's third dream. Alerted in one final dream, they made a long and arduous journey instead to Nazareth in Galilee to escape the threat posed by Herod's ruling son Archelaus. In each instance, Joseph acted courageously. During a pilgrimage to Jerusalem years later he and Mary anxiously sought their lost twelve-year old son. *(Similarly, we recall our sudden apprehension when our five-year-old daughter wandered away at a church festival. What a relief to find her on the edge of the crowd!)*

Nowhere do the Gospels report Joseph saying a single word. Though presented as a quiet man, he acts with a resolute determination. His power is grounded in a radical trust of divine providence whose plan far exceeded what he could comprehend. How might he have expressed his consternation about Mary's pregnancy, his concern for the shame that acquaintances from the village may have heaped upon them, or his fears for the safety of his wife and child? He never explains.

This story of Joseph recalls the life of another dreamer, the Joseph of Genesis whose dreams and ability to interpret the dreams of others led to his rise to power in Pharaoh's court (Genesis 37:1–11, 41:1–45). Both Josephs had a father named Jacob; both took decisive action during a time of crisis. Dreams to these men are revelatory, making known the divine plan. That is how God mysteriously communicated with them.

The Man in the Shadows

The last time Joseph appears on the scene is when he and Mary found Jesus in the temple and were astonished at their twelve-year-old child's impressive understanding demonstrated among the teachers (Luke 2:41–51). From this we can conclude that Mary and Joseph shared at least twelve years of marriage. During that time Jesus would have learned much about life from his parents. They would have modeled for him the intimacy of human connection and the tender love of God. Nothing is known about when Joseph died or the grief his wife and son experienced. He is not mentioned with Mary at the foot of the cross or when she is in the upper room with the apostles after the resurrection (Acts 1:12–14).

Our artist friend David, who is preparing to write an icon of Joseph, views Joseph as a loving, obedient, courageous, and working father, yet one who is in the shadows of his son. David comments, "a father in the shadows intrigues me most." He further reflects that Joseph could easily have said no to marrying Mary, "but he did not, and that courage and obedience to God and then to step back in the shadows is what I admire in him. I often wonder if he and Mary ever discussed all of this among themselves."

Let It Be

Let's go back now and pick up Mary's side of the story. For this we go to Luke's account of the angel Gabriel who came to Mary (Luke 1:26–38).

> Gabriel: "Greetings, favored one! The Lord is with you."

Mary "was much perplexed by his words and pondered," What's he talking about?

Gabriel: "Do not be afraid, Mary, for you have found favor with God. And now, you will conceive in your womb and bear a son, and you will name him Jesus."

Mary: "How can this be, since I am a virgin?"

Gabriel: "The Holy Spirit will come upon you, and the power of the Most High will overshadow you; therefore the child to be born will be holy; he will be called the Son of God. . . . For nothing will be impossible with God."

Mary: "Here am I, the servant of the Lord; let it be [Latin *fiat*] with me according to your word."

This short exchange with a surprise visitor turned the life of a young peasant woman upside down. She engages in direct dialogue with God's messenger and is not afraid to ask how a virgin not yet having "known" a man can become pregnant; amazingly she freely consents to participate in this radical, divine plan. According to theologian Elizabeth Johnson, "this event actually subverts patriarchy by replacing the usual male participation with *ruah*, the creative Spirit of God."[25] Mary's affirmative response to her mysterious, humanly incomprehensible situation recalls the popular song, "Let it Be" (1970), written and sung by Paul McCartney of the Beatles:

> When I find myself in times of trouble, Mother Mary comes to me
>
> Speaking words of wisdom, let it be
>
> And in my hour of darkness, she is standing right in front of me
>
> Speaking words of wisdom, let it be

The inspiration for the lyrics came to McCartney during a tense period when he had a dream about his own mother Mary who died some years earlier. In an interview he said that his mother had told him, "It will be all right, just let it be." One can hear this song with biblical overtones.

In contrast to the many famous artists and iconographers of the Annunciation who portray Mary with regal attire in a palatial setting, it is important to keep in mind that in Luke the angel appeared to a poor peasant woman living in the hamlet of Nazareth. It is notable that in her reported apparitions throughout Christian history, Mary was experienced as appearing to people in poor circumstances and therefore has become a source of strength for those in similar situations.

A Pregnant Woman at the Border

In late November 2020 an exhausted Griselda arrived at the border between Mexico and the United States 38 weeks pregnant.[26] After crossing the Rio Grande she was sent back to Mexico, where she gave birth to a tiny daughter. Not unlike the situation of Mary and Joseph who found that "there was no place for them in the inn" (Luke 2:7), Griselda experienced what another woman was told by a U.S. Customs and Border Protection agent: the President "doesn't want there to be any more pregnant people here." Many of these women had journeyed for days, often paying smugglers large amounts of money along the way.

Expectant Mothers Coming Together

While some have debated from a biological perspective how Mary became pregnant, Barbara Reid and Shelly Matthews explain that "Luke's intent is not to convey the historical circumstances of Jesus's birth but to make a theological and Christological assertion."[27] Luke emphasizes that Jesus' origin arises from "the power of the Most High," exercised through the Holy Spirit (1:35). Once she becomes aware of her pregnancy, and possibly prompted by swirling gossip in the small village of Nazareth, it is easy to understand why she leaves town and hastily travels to Judea to spend time with her older relative Elizabeth who is also pregnant. One young expectant mother seeks out the comfort, nurture, and wisdom of another, a wise mentor, who herself is also dealing with a surprise pregnancy. Mutually supportive, they serve as a model to circles of women today, including immigrant, abandoned, and unwed mothers, who seek companionship and guidance, drawing upon one another's strength.

Upon Mary's arrival Elizabeth welcomes her with an enthusiastic "Blessed are you among women," a greeting echoed later in the Gospel by an unnamed woman who praises Mary's motherhood: "Blessed is the womb that bore you and the breasts that nursed you!" (Luke 11:27). Jesus redirects the blessing in terms of discipleship. Like her namesake Miriam, a prophetess in the Old Testament who with other women led the Israelites in song and dance (Exodus 15:20–21), Mary responds to Elizabeth in a prophetic canticle known as the Magnificat (Luke 1:46–55). Mary, who would have experienced first-hand the dominant grip of the power brokers, the economic exploitation of the villagers, and the hunger pangs of the poor, acclaims the blessings brought by the power of God.

Mary's public proclamation, something usually done only by men, is a prelude to the reversal of fortunes announced later by her son in beatitudes and parables. Those previously enthroned, secure in their riches, and satiated at banquets are put on notice that God, through a manifestation of divine strength, has far different priorities. With such courageous speech, Mary demonstrates strength and a profound faith in the saving action of God.

Family Issues

When Joseph and Mary reported for the census in Bethlehem, "the time came for her to deliver her child" and "she gave birth to her firstborn son" (Luke 2:6–7). Did Jesus have siblings? In Mark 6:3, where Jesus is identified as the "brother" of James, Joses, Judas, and Simon as well as having "sisters," the most probable answer historically is yes. Since at least the patristic period, it has been argued whether these are full siblings, half siblings or cousins of Jesus. The official teaching of the Catholic Church, as outlined in the *Catechism*, is that Jesus is Mary's only son, and that Mary was a perpetual virgin; "brothers" is to be interpreted not as "blood brothers," but more generally as "close relations of Jesus" (#500, 501). In contrast, the traditional Protestant interpretation is to take the text literally as blood siblings. Reflecting that there is still debate from an historical angle if not doctrinal, Roman Catholic scripture scholar John P. Meier argues that the term "brothers" is to be interpreted as full brothers of Jesus (see also John 2:12; 7:3).[28] Whatever the case, Joseph and Mary likely had their hands full as parents providing for the family, managing sibling squabbles, and keeping them safe from external danger.

A crisis point was reached after Jesus left home and began roaming the countryside, confronting unclean spirits, and fomenting tension with the religious authorities. When his family got wind of this, some thought he had "gone out of his mind," and his family "went out to restrain him" (Mark 3:21). How this strain between mother (Joseph is not mentioned) and son is worked out and resolved, if it was, is not indicated in the text. Either way, this tension in the family did not prevent Mary from being present at the agonizing death of her Son.

The Anguish of a Parent at the Death of a Child

Indeed, the Gospel of John takes particular care to portray the mother of Jesus standing at the foot of the cross (John 19:25–27). Her posture of standing demonstrates an inner strength in the midst of tremendous grief. There she witnesses one of the most excruciating events a mother can possibly imagine: the torturous death of her Son, an innocent person put to death as a criminal. This brings to mind grief-stricken mothers and grandmothers throughout the world who have suffered the loss of their sons through totalitarian regimes; for example, during the "dirty war" in the 1970s in Argentina, through terrorist groups like ISIS today who behead some captives, and through targeting and indiscriminate killing by street gangs. To all these, Mary may serve as a source of comfort, joining them in their suffering. Michelangelo captures this poignant pain in his iconic *Pietà*, portraying a youthful appearing Mary holding on her lap the battered, lifeless body of her Son.

Curiously, in the intimate exchange on the cross, Jesus refers to his mother somewhat impersonally as "Woman," not by her name or her relationship to him, when he commends her to the beloved disciple: "Woman, here is your son" (John 19:26). "Woman" is the way Jesus typically addresses women in John's Gospel (and periodically in the Synoptics; see Matthew 15:28). Never mentioning Mary by name, the evangelist refers to her as "the mother of Jesus" or simply "his mother" (2:1, 3, 5, 12; 6:42; 19:25–27). This is not disrespectful but stylistic.

In an earlier instance, after Jesus' mother brings to his attention the depleted wine at the wedding at Cana, he addresses her with what sounds to our ears like a sharp reprimand: "Woman, what concern is that to you and to me?" (John 2:4). While this may be considered "a normal, polite form of address" (see 4:21) as noted by the New American Bible, it may indicate more specifically that the emphasis here is on Jesus as his Father's Son (5:25–38) rather than his mother's child. Others suggest that the epithet "Woman" has a symbolic meaning, recalling the creation of the first woman (Genesis 2:23–24), the "new Eve" in the language of some patristic and medieval interpretations. In any case, Mary persists, not taking no for an answer: "Do whatever he tells you" (2:5). Going against the grain of her culture's ideal of femininity, she does not stay silent or remain submissive to her son's dismissal of her concern.[29] Rather, her persuasiveness prompts Jesus to perform "the first of his signs" (2:11). Both in the Magnificat and at Cana Mary's assertiveness plays a key role in advancing God's plan.

To conclude, the story of Joseph shows how this man, in the words of Ron Rolheiser, "can be a pious believer, deeply faithful to everything within his religious tradition, and yet at the same time be open to a mystery beyond both his human and religious understanding."[30] Joseph took risks, demonstrated commitment to his wife who was faced with very compromising circumstances, and trusted divine guidance that came to him through dreams. He is fittingly called a just and upright man.

For her part, Mary is presented as the model of discipleship. She faced the daunting predicament of her unexpected pregnancy, found acceptance and companionship with her husband Joseph, and endured suffering. She stands out as a prophet and a friend of God, the mother to all those who are inspired by the way she lived her life as a faithful woman.

For Reflection:

- In what ways have Mary and Joseph become role models for believers and for you specifically?
- What are some unexpected experiences of God's presence in your life that stand out for you?

Chapter Four

Mothers and Fathers of the Tribes

In this chapter we will enter the world of the patriarchs and matriarchs of Israel, the latter of whom remain largely in the shadows of the former. In paying close attention to the dynamics between these men and women, it may be instructive, some suggest, to view their lives through the lens of the contemporary #MeToo Movement.

As a frequent refrain in the Bible, we often hear the Holy One described in the traditional credal statement: "the God of Abraham, Isaac, and Jacob" (such as Genesis 50:24; Exodus 3:15; Acts 3:13, 7:32). This same formula is also commonly used by Jews in daily prayers. Three generations of men are named as progenitors; neither their wives nor their concubines are mentioned in this covenantal formula of faith. It is true that throughout the Bible God is intimately involved in the lives of humankind. However, is this God a God only of men? What about the God of Sarah, Rebekah, Rachel, and Leah? What is the merit of these and other women who played essential roles in the story of Israel?

We are also mindful of a very different context, where the Gospel of Mark reports that Jesus fed five thousand *men* in the miracle of the loaves and fishes (6:35–44). Again the women, who surely were also nourished, are invisible in the count. Maybe the simple answer is that these accounts are androcentric, by men writing in a man's world. As we dip back into the world of the patriarchs and matriarchs, let's take a closer look at how males and females are portrayed in their masculinity and femininity, mindful that there is a certain fluidity at times in how they are constructed and presented by the biblical authors.[31]

Masculinity on Full Display

Abram, a name changed later to Abraham, is privileged as the chosen founder of "a great nation" to be called Israel. He was a landowner with male and female slaves; he was rich in livestock, gold, and silver (Genesis 13:2). The first among the patriarchs, he exercises leadership by moving his family and possessions from northwestern Mesopotamia along the typical migration route to the land of Canaan. He is a good provider, but essentially a migrant, seeking food during a time of famine; he recognizes his wife as a "woman beautiful in appearance" (12:11).

When three mysterious visitors appear, Abraham extends hospitality by the oaks of Mamre. In contrast, his wife Sarah, to whom Abraham goes back and forth during the encounter, remains in the tent (18:1–15)—in ancient Middle Eastern societies, a man's place is the public arena and a woman's is the private living space. Abraham is also adept in warfare—we see him defeat the kings who captured his relative Lot (chapter 14). He is a skilled debater, persuading someone no less than God to adjust the numbers regarding the planned destruction of Sodom and Gomorrah (18:16–33). All of these are praiseworthy masculine qualities.

Whose Son "Counts" as the Heir?

Yet Abraham fell short in other areas. He was paternalistic toward women; on two occasions he endangered his wife Sarai (whose name was later changed to Sarah). Twice he disowned her, passing her off as his sister to save his own skin. When he initially failed to father offspring by Sarah—as promised by God—he shifted the blame to her. He later banished his intended heir Ishmael along with his mother Hagar to the desert with few provisions. And he was surprisingly passive, uttering no protest, when God incomprehensibly commanded him to slay Isaac, his first-born son from Sarah. There are both admirable as well as oppressive and unsavory qualities to Abraham's masculinity. Is he a "real" man or not?

Already from the start of the patriarchal narratives, in the Abraham saga, a masculinity that dominates and subordinates is being redefined. Susan Haddox explains: "One of the primary characteristics of 'biblical' masculinity" is that "submission to God outweighs the 'normal' expectations of masculine behavior."[32]

Compared to Abraham, the story of Isaac is sketchier. Favored over his half-brother Ishmael, who was foretold to become "a wild ass of a man" (Genesis 16:12), Isaac plays either an astonishingly trustful or else a very passive role in his own near-sacrifice by his father (chapter 22), whether out of fear or perhaps sheer parental obedience. He mourns the death of his mother Sarah and prays for his barren wife Rebekah (25:21). The narrative does not present the infertility as his issue, for this would have been a slight to his manhood. Following the pattern of his father, when they must travel to escape famine, Isaac passes his wife off as his sister because he is afraid the men would kill him for her (26:6–11), a questionable way of manifesting his honor as a man. He became very wealthy and powerful, too much so for the neighboring king Abimelech. His riches might rank him among the top tier of wealthy biblical characters, along with others such as Solomon and the man with "many possessions" who encounters Jesus (Mark 10:17–22).

Deception and Blessing

Over against the towering stature of his father and grandfather, Jacob appears as the first of several "younger and less typically masculine son[s] who [are] favored."[33] In a prenatal skirmish in the womb, Jacob held onto the heel of his slightly older brother Esau, and so he received the name *Jacob,* coming either from the Hebrew term meaning "to follow" or "to come behind," or the term meaning "heel"—hardly admirable qualities for a male (Genesis 25:19–34).

Unlike his twin Esau, a skillful hunter, Jacob was a homebody, "a quiet man" with "smooth skin" (25:27, 27:11).

When Jacob conspired with his mother through trickery to steal the birthright from Esau given through Jacob's blessing perhaps she was remembering a prediction she had heard before the boys' birth: "Two nations are in your womb, and two peoples born of you shall be divided; the one shall be stronger than the other, the elder shall serve the younger" (Gen 25:23). Esau afterward became angry and wanted to kill Jacob. Soon after deceiving his father, Jacob flees for his life, becoming a fugitive living in fear of Esau. Esau's threat of violence recalls Cain's violent murder of his brother Abel out of jealousy.

Esau, of course, did not kill Jacob, for Jacob went on to father twelve sons and one daughter by four women: Leah, who became his wife through deception; the slave women Bilhah and Zilpah; and his beloved wife Rachel. With a touch of Hollywood staging, Jacob, Leah, and Rachel became the Bible's classic love triangle. This complicated situation was set up when Jacob was tricked by his father-in-law into marrying Leah, the sister of his true love Rachel, because she was the older sister.

The Wounded Wrestler

One night, while on his way to reconcile with his brother Esau, Jacob sent his wives and concubines away. He wrestled with an unidentified man until daybreak (Genesis

32:24–32). Although this man did not prevail against Jacob, he struck Jacob's hip socket, putting it out of joint. His male body is wounded, having suffered a crippling attack. After the unarmed non-lethal combat, the man reveals his identity, explaining to the injured Jacob that he had been grappling "with God [in physical form] and with humans." The prophet Hosea explains the incident as Jacob contending "in his manhood" with God (Hosea 12:3). Although having suffered an injury that left him limping, Jacob persists in striving against the man and later realizes: "I have seen God face to face, and yet my life is preserved."

As the story concludes, it appears that Jacob has prevailed over God and human beings. Curiously, this is the only instance in the Bible when a blessing was procured in the aftermath of a struggle. Just before the blessing, Jacob is given the name *Israel* (Hebrew for "God strives"), which then becomes the tribal name of the people divided into male-centric lineages headed by his twelve sons. The people of Israel, after Jacob's time, will face multiple struggles: slavery, wandering in the desert, settling the land promised by God, being conquered and carried off into exile, returning to a destroyed city, and being refashioned by the God who called them.

Looking back through Jacob's life one can ask if there was an up-side to Jacob's early and less-than-noble deception of Esau? Frederick Buechner believes there is. He puts it in these words: "The shrewd and ambitious man who is strong on guts and weak on conscience, who knows very well what he wants and directs all his energies toward getting it, the Jacobs of this world, all in all do pretty well."[34] Does this mean we should guide our children to become more Jacobs in this world in this sense? Certainly not. Rather, it reflects the fact that in all the messy situations humans seem inevitably to bring about, God is present, often in ways that are not immediately understood.

Our Fathers, Our Selves

Jacob encounters God in his vulnerability. This opens up the question of the relationship between masculinity and vulnerability. Can they exist side by side? Men who dare to tap into their vulnerability, their insecurity, and their limitations often find a new personal freedom when they no longer have to wear the mask of always being in control, dominating subordinates, and exercising power. Male vulnerability may involve facing what has been called one's "father wounds," arising from experiences ranging from lack of validation to outright rejection. These emotional wounds are those that a person may have experienced due to the shortcomings of one's own father, authority figures, or religious leaders. Healing is often a gradual process facilitated by interactions with a counselor, companionship with adult males, and/or retreat-like experiences led by a trusted guide.

In his weekly audience on June 10, 2020, Pope Francis reflected on Jacob's all-night struggle with God and compared it to prayer. He said that prayer is not always easy and may mean fighting with God. His message is that prayer demands that we struggle with God and recognize our weakness and frailty before God.[35] Undoubtedly Saint Paul also wrestled with God, as he came to grips with his enigmatic thorn in the flesh, perhaps a sickness or a physical disability, that a "messenger of Satan" used to torment him. Three times he appealed to the Lord that the thorn would leave him, evidently to no avail. Instead he received this consolation: "My grace is sufficient for you, for power is made perfect in weakness" (2 Corinthians 12:7–9). Jesus too experienced anguish just before his excruciating death, when he prayed that God would remove his cup of suffering, but then submitted himself completely to the will of the Father (Mark 14:34–36).

On a spiritual level, interpreters have viewed the wrestling match between God and Jacob as the latter coming to terms with his misdeeds: stealing his brother's birthright and deceiving his father so as to obtain his blessing. In moments of clarity—the "appointment with God," perhaps in "moments of disorientation" described by the pope—men today may grasp the action needed to make a course correction in their lives as they wrestle with their past.

> *As a hospital chaplain, John has witnessed how much relief it brings, for example, when an abusive father seeks forgiveness from a daughter whom he victimized.*

After the wrestling, Jacob no longer has an unblemished male body. One scholar explains that in the Hebrew Bible "the image of the abled body reflects the idea of a perfect body made in the image of God."[36] Later in Israel it was assumed that the king would have a body robust enough so that he could lead the people into battle (1 Samuel 8:19–20). This was not the case, for example, with Saul's grandson, Mephibosheth, the next in line to become king, who, having become crippled at age five, was not a threat to David's kingship (2 Samuel 4). In our modern world, extensive media coverage no longer allows leaders to mask their physical vulnerabilities. Consider President Franklin D. Roosevelt, who went to great lengths to prevent any photography showing his difficulty in walking due to his polio-ravaged body. Did he fear his physical weakness would have a negative impact on the perception of his manhood and his ability to be seen as a strong leader?

David, on the other hand, embodied masculinity in several aspects: as a skilled warrior responsible for killing thousands, as a powerful king, through his leadership ability, by his "verbal prowess and persuasiveness," in his handsome appearance and attraction to women, and by his bonding with other men, notably Jonathan.[37] In contrast, in 2 Kings chapter 11, there is an account of a warrior queen, Athaliah, who reigned for seven years. Challenging gender boundaries, she is portrayed as a wicked ruler, perhaps in part for having challenged the submissive role of women. On the other hand, David's masculinity seems compromised due to his moral failures and his inability to discipline his children or exercise control over his kingdom.[38] Manifesting his softer side, David was deeply moved and wept at the death of his son Absalom (2 Samuel

18:33), recalling the several times that Jacob's son Joseph wept, particularly at his father's death (Genesis 50:1).

David's relationship with Jonathan is portrayed as particularly close. The "soul of Jonathan was bound to the soul of David"; the two "kissed each other, and wept with each other," and at Jonathan's death, David laments: "your love to me was wonderful, / passing the love of women" (1 Samuel 18:1, 20:41; 2 Samuel 1:26). While some may read homoerotic tensions into this narrative, the text does not convey evidence of a homosexual relationship.[39]

From these founding fathers and the great King David, we have seen a wide scope of masculinity ranging from robust actions and military prowess to struggle and vulnerability. In the Book of Proverbs, an alternate model of masculinity emerges that moves away from a manhood based on physical strength to one centered on inner strength and patience (e.g., Proverbs 25:15), qualities that are manifest in the lives of Jesus and Paul, for example. With this overview of masculinities, we transition now to the matriarchs and the femininity they embody.

The Matriarchs Step into the Limelight

Sarah, the lawful wife of Abraham and known for her beauty, was the first matriarch. Her name means "princess." God promised Abraham that she would bear a son and that "she shall give rise to nations; kings of peoples shall come from her" (Genesis 17:15–16). She and Abraham are closely related; in fact they are siblings, having different mothers but the same father (20:12). This explains why Abraham is able to claim her as both wife and sister.

In the patriarchal system, a woman is defined by her ability to have a son. Called Sarai ("put above") until her name was changed to Sarah, she was barren (Genesis 11:30, 16:1). Frustrated with God's apparent lack of help, she took matters into her own hands and offered her Egyptian slave-woman Hagar to Abram so that she, Sarah, "shall obtain children by her" (16:2). In exercising agency, Sarah tells Abraham twice what to do, but Hagar has no say in the situation. Paul refers to both Abraham's own body being "as good as dead" as well as "the barrenness of Sarah's womb" as a way of accentuating Abraham's faith (Romans 4:19). In his Letter to the Galatians, Paul likens Sarah to "the Jerusalem above" and calls her "our mother" (Galatians 4:26). She becomes the mother of all children of the promise, not only of Isaac.

Back in Genesis, however, the picture is not so exalted. When Hagar does bear a son, Sarah lashes out at Abraham: "May the wrong done to me be on you!" (16:5). In the face of this perceived injustice, Sarah takes the low road; she becomes angry, jealous, and vindictive toward Hagar and her son Ishmael. The reader might be shocked that the free woman Sarah could be brutally unfeeling toward the young enslaved woman and her son, after Sarah herself gave her to her husband. But the narrator seems unsurprised at Sarah's actions; we are not told how these disagreeable qualities were perceived by those around her. Were they considered negative aspects of femininity? Sarah's range of feminine qualities is even more hidden in the account of Abraham's excruciating experience of God telling him to sacrifice their son Isaac. Sarah's role and Isaac's attitude toward his father during and after being spared as a sacrifice are lost in the story.

You Did What?

Did Abraham tell Sarah ahead of time about his decision to obey God and sacrifice Isaac? (Genesis 22:1–19) Or, was Abraham nowhere near Sarah at the time of God's demand? Would she have agreed? If not, did Abraham cavalierly dismiss whatever she might have thought about God's challenge to him? How did Isaac feel after the whole experience? What was it like to know your father was willing to kill you to please God? These probing questions hint at why the sacrifice of Isaac, also called the *Aqedah* ("binding") in Hebrew, has become an absorbing archetypal story that has fascinated readers over the centuries.

Ironically, Sarah had far more to lose than did Abraham if Isaac died. She had only this child, whom we assume she loved but also whose very existence validated her place as Abraham's wife, the matriarch of his people, the mother of his heir. Abraham, however, who had exiled Ishmael, probably still had many other competitive sons from his concubines (Genesis 25:1–6), which was a standard practice at the time.

Sarah may have felt cautious about trusting the God whose prolonged silence she had endured before he kept his covenantal promise and answered her prayers, so it's hard to imagine that she might have acquiesced to the divine request for Isaac's life. It's a guess, of course, but it's easy to suspect she had no idea, and thus no chance to protest what Abraham intended to do in the land of Moriah. How shocked she must have been when he then returned with Isaac and told her what he had *almost* done. "Could you tell me that again? You almost did what?"

Female (and Male) Trickery

The quality of seizing the initiative within her cultural limitations as a woman comes to the fore in the story of the next matriarch, Rebekah. Abraham had sent his servant back to Nahor in Mesopotamia to find a wife for Isaac, and the Lord led him to Rebekah, who "was very fair to look upon" (Genesis 24:16). She was beautiful, like Sarah, and like Sarah, she took the initiative within the parameters of her patriarchal marriage to get her own way. She tricked her old and blind husband Isaac into giving his blessing to her favored son Jacob rather than to his slightly older twin brother Esau. This of course unleashed fury on the part of Esau and injected a spirit of hatred and division into Rebekah's family. Nevertheless, like her mother-in-law Sarah, she demonstrates that clever manipulation was a female technique that enabled women to gain some power within their cultural confines—even if it contributed to pain and anger within their families.

Feminine trickery is also exhibited by Lot's daughters (who got their father drunk so they could have sexual relations with him; Genesis 19:30–38), Rachel (who stole her father's household gods to defy her father's control; 31:1–21), and Tamar (who disguised herself as a prostitute; chapter 38). These women exercised their power not with brute force but by using their courage, intelligence, sexuality, and deceit to accomplish their goals. Though women in the patriarchal world had little power in a formal or legal sense, they applied their ingenuity to assert some control of at least some aspects of their daily lives and destinies. The art of trickery was certainly one way women could have the last word, at least occasionally.

The theme of trickery resurfaces, this time male-initiated, in the story of Laban and his daughters (Genesis chapter 29). Jacob's true love was Rachel, yet Laban wanted to marry off his older daughter Leah first. When the time for marriage came, Laban deceived Jacob by giving him Leah as his wife instead of Rachel. Leah felt afflicted and hoped to gain Jacob's love by bearing children, but to no avail. Rachel, who later became Jacob's second wife, was barren and jealous of Leah.

Unwanted? On Hold? No Tricks Left?

It appears certain that the matriarchal women we have mentioned had very little say about whose wife (thus property) they became. Looking back especially at Leah and Rachel, we can ask: How did Leah feel to have been secretly foisted upon Jacob—and to know he was disappointed? How did she feel when he nevertheless used her to give him many sons? How did Rachel, who must have already been of marriageable age for seven years when that happened, react? Rachel, along with Jacob, demonstrated extraordinary endurance waiting so many years to tie the knot with him—years in which she might have had many children.

These women, whose true feelings we can only guess, must have had a strong sense of long-suffering patience with their lot. Even from beneath the veneer of androcentric narratives their grief seems apparent. When Rachel finally became the mother of Joseph and then Benjamin, at whose birth she died, how great must have been her joy, but also her sorrow as she so soon left them in death. Those earlier potentially life-giving years lost in waiting for Jacob to marry her could not have been erased from her memory. In later centuries the prophet Jeremiah (31:15) described Rachel weeping for her children as a metaphor of grief for the tribes going into exile. Was that because she had long been a model for the profound grief of women for whom motherhood had been unreachable, delayed, frustrated, or terminated by death? Matthew also (2:18) followed Jeremiah in referring to Rachel's weeping for her children, so deep a grief "she refused to be consoled."

In sum, a range of masculinity and femininity are on full display among Israel's founding fathers and mothers. Some traits are laudable, others not. A masculinity that dominates and subordinates is being redefined, outweighed by the expectation to submit to God. On the feminine side, subordination to men remains the norm, yet women find a way to exercise agency and accomplish some of their purposes. How remarkable that throughout the course of human history, God works in and through women and men, with all their foibles, brokenness, and vulnerabilities.

For Reflection:

- What are some of the most and least admirable qualities of the matriarchs and patriarchs from the perspective of sex?
- When have you wrestled with God over important decisions or how to express your femininity or masculinity?

Chapter Five

Women and Men in the Shadows

We all know individuals who are somewhat hidden. Perhaps they are shy or timid, and thus easily overlooked. Diving deeper into the Scriptures, we now turn to lesser-known men and women, those who often receive little attention. We are not searching for ideal types, for they hardly exist. Instead, our intention is to bring to the surface an array of persons who witness to the wide spectrum of humanity through whom God works. The first part of our remarks will be devoted to the four women from the Old Testament who make a surprising appearance in the genealogy of Jesus (Matthew 1:1–17). Each of them finds a way to exert some power in a man's world, and thus to challenge the dominant masculinity. The four women are colorful characters: Tamar and Rahab are prostitutes, Ruth is an outsider, and the wife of Uriah was caught up in an adulterous affair. We will also look at some of the men in their lives.

The latter part of the chapter will focus on some less familiar New Testament figures of authority and power whose political roles brought them into contact with John the Baptist and Paul. They form two groups of political personalities: Herod Antipas, Herodias, and Salome; and Bernice and Agrippa. These influential powerbrokers are intriguing characters in their own right who had a significant impact on early Christian history.

The More Righteous Prostitute and the Son of Jacob

The story of Tamar, a young Canaanite woman, begins with Judah, one of Jacob's sons (Genesis chapter 38). Judah found Tamar as a wife for his oldest son Er, whom the Lord later killed for his wickedness. Following the custom that would become Levirate marriage (Deuteronomy 25:5–10), Jacob then gave Tamar to his second son Onan, whom the Lord also killed for misdeeds. But then—evidently blaming Tamar for being the killer-wife—Judah refused to give her to his youngest son Shelah fearing that he also might die.

Some time later Tamar learns that Judah will be passing by her father's house, and she jumps into action. Disguised as a prostitute, she waits at the town's entrance aware that Judah is in the area. As a childless widow and prostitute out on the road, she is doubly marginalized. In this socially suspect situation, she, like many before and after her, used trickery to gain power. Driven by desire, Judah solicits her, promising a kid goat in return. Tamar shrewdly asks for a pledge until the goat is sent, and he obliges, giving her his signet, cord, and staff. When Judah later discovers that his daughter-in-law, though living as a widow, is pregnant, he demands: "Bring her out, and let her be burned" (38:24).

When Tamar is brought out to be executed, she sends word to her father-in-law that "it was the owner of these [pledges] who made me pregnant" (38:25). She had wisely held on to the signet, cord, and staff he gave her, as a way of retaining power over him and ensuring that she would be given what she was owed. Like his grandfather Isaac, Judah was tricked by a woman's craftiness. Seeing the evidence, Judah had little choice but to acknowledge that he was the perpetrator and then to accept the legal consequences since "if a man lies with his daughter-in-law, both of them shall be put to death" (Leviticus 20:12). Judah then, acknowledging his complicity in the situation, confesses: "She is more in the right than I, since I did not give her to my son Shelah" (38:26). Putting righteousness on a relative scale, he recognizes that Tamar's actions were more moral than his. Although Tamar is not exonerated, Judah recognizes that her goodness exceeds his own. Still, Tamar stands out as the only woman in the Old Testament who is called righteous. That puts her on a level with Elizabeth, who stands alone among women in the New Testament as "righteous before God" (Luke 1:6).

In due time, Tamar gives birth to twins, Perez and Zerah, fathered by Judah, yet she evidently remains a single mother. Through these sons, she saves Judah's household, and is herself named as an ancestor of David and ultimately of Jesus himself. Can you imagine how the conversation might unfold if Jesus were invited to comment on his family tree? In the biblical tale of Tamar she is rewarded for her role, and her feminine power is celebrated.

Judah's interaction with Tamar is only one dimension of his family problems. Earlier he, along with most of his brothers, alienated and hated his brother Joseph. Judah is the one who suggested selling Joseph to the Ishmaelites; he this did, however, to save Joseph from being killed by his brothers (Genesis 37:26–28). Before Jacob's death, he blesses Judah as a strong warrior, noting that his brothers would bow down to him, that he would be "a lion's whelp," and that the scepter would not depart from him (49:8–10). The tribe named after him became very important in the unfolding history of the Israelites. The New Testament records that the Lord (Jesus) is descended from Judah (Hebrews 7:14; see also Matthew's and Luke's genealogies) and that Jesus himself is the "Lion of the tribe of Judah" (Revelation 5:5). Even though Judah failed in fulfilling his responsibilities to Tamar, his reputation did not prevent Jesus himself from being identified with his characteristic trademark, that of the lion. The tribal identity of Jesus as a Judahite transcended the sins of his ancestors.

The Faithful Prostitute, the Warrior, and the Spies

To modern sensibilities, a "faithful prostitute" appears to be a classic oxymoron. Rahab is assigned this descriptor in a contemporary devotional where she is included as an example of the "Blessed Among Us."[40] The Canaanite Rahab appears on the scene as Joshua prepares for the conquest of Jericho (Joshua 2:1–21, 6:15–25). He sent spies who "entered the house of a prostitute whose name was

Rahab" (2:1). Nothing is said in the Bible about whether the spies entered into a relationship with Rahab. For her part, Rahab showed tremendous courage in deciding to hide them within her house in the city wall, protecting them from the men sent by the king of Jericho.

Rahab recounts to the scouts the saving deeds she has heard that the Lord accomplished. She professes: "The LORD your God is indeed God in heaven above and on earth below" (2:11). Then she strikes a bargain, asking them to swear to protect her and her family when the Israelites storm the city. Agreeing, the spies instruct her to tie a crimson cord in her window to guarantee the family's safety during the city's destruction. She helps them escape by letting them down by a rope through the window. After Jericho falls to the Israelites, we are told that Rahab's family "lived in Israel ever since" (6:25).

In his genealogy of Jesus, Matthew identifies Rahab, a marginalized outsider, as the mother of Boaz by Salmon (Matthew 1:5). The author of Hebrews includes "Rahab the prostitute" among the cloud of witnesses, praising her faith along with that of such notables as the patriarchs and Moses. Hebrews explains that she did not perish with the disobedient because by faith she "had received the spies in peace" (11:31). Similarly, the Letter of James asserts that she was "justified by works" (James 2:25). We don't hear a word of rebuke for her role as a prostitute. Rather, this woman is held up as a model of faith.

Later rabbinic tradition presented Rahab as a convert to Judaism and the wife of Joshua. They had daughters but no sons. Both Joshua and Rahab are mentioned in Dante's *Divine Comedy* (around AD 1320). The poet refers to Joshua in passing but highlights Rahab as virtuous, a bright star, "the first to rise among the souls redeemed in Christ's great triumph," and the one who "made possible Joshua's first glory" (*Paradise* 9.112–126).[41] The city prostitute outshines the victorious warrior, a subversion of both historical values and the sex hierarchy.

A Poor Foreign Widow and a Rich Native Landowner

The story of Ruth is often cast as a love story, but it is much more. The tale begins with a family from Bethlehem who left their homeland due to famine, and who encounter Ruth and Orpah, young non-Hebrew women of Moab. The narrator recounts how the family's two sons, Mahlon and Chilion, "took" these women as their wives (Ruth 1:4). Based on a close analysis of the Hebrew verb (*nsh'*) some argue persuasively that this was a "rape-marriage."[42] In what appears to be a similar case, the Book of Judges (which immediately precedes the Book of Ruth) ends with the scandalous account of young men from the tribe of Benjamin who "carry off" as wives for themselves the young women of Shiloh who were dancing in the festival (Judges 21:15–24). The NRSV interprets this in a note as "the rape of the daughters of Shiloh."

After Mahlon and Chilion die without offspring, Ruth, now a widow, faithfully accompanies her bereft mother-in-law Naomi back to her home territory of Judah. Ruth pledges her allegiance to Naomi in a heartfelt speech that begins: "Where you go, I will go; / where you lodge, I will lodge; / your people shall be my people, / and your God my God" (1:16). This inspiring passage is often read at weddings. Sometimes people are surprised to find out that these words were spoken from a daughter-in-law to her mother-in law!

Because of the close relationship between Ruth and Naomi, this verse is also sometimes adopted by same-sex gender couples as a blessing. Along those lines, the character Ruth in the movie *Fried Green Tomatoes* sends her female friend Idgie "the text of Ruth 1:16 to inform her about her desire to leave her abusive husband and live with her."[43]

The women reach Bethlehem at harvest time. As they struggle to survive, Ruth takes the initiative, asking Naomi: "Let me go to the field and glean among the ears of grain, behind someone in whose sight I may find favor" (2:2). That "someone" turned out to be Naomi's relative Boaz, a prominent rich man, the son of Rahab.

Ruth's gleaning calls to mind the famous 1857 painting *The Gleaners* by Jean-François Millet, now on display in the Musée d'Orsay in Paris. Much social controversy was inspired by this portrayal of three French peasant women doing the back-breaking work of gleaning wheat from the stubble left behind by the harvesters. The painting was seen as threatening to middle and upper classes, who, feeling echoes of the French Revolution, feared it as a glorification of the peasants.

Thousands of years earlier, Ruth's gleaning, in contrast, was looked upon benignly and protectively by the owner of the field, Boaz. Indeed, he takes notice, inquires about the identity of his gleaner, and instructs the young men not to bother her. He is aware that Ruth is a potential target for sexual harassment. Ruth wonders: "Why have I found favor in your sight, that you should take notice of me, when I am a foreigner?" (2:10).

Boaz, impressed with all that Ruth has done for her mother-in-law, offers this blessing: "May the Lord reward you for your deeds, and may you have a full reward from the Lord, the God of Israel, under whose wings you have come for refuge!" (2:12). His blessings continue the next time they meet: "May you be blessed by the Lord, my daughter; this last instance of your loyalty is better than the first; you have not gone after young men, whether poor or rich" (3:10). He sees Ruth as "a worthy woman" (3:11). Much to his credit, Boaz, a man of privilege, offers support and protection; he listens to, blesses, and affirms this foreign woman who, no doubt to his surprise, finds her way not only to his bountiful harvest but also to his bedside at night on the threshing floor.

Naomi and Ruth had devised a daring plan. Ruth was to go to the threshing floor at night and surreptitiously lay at the feet of Boaz, whom she believes is her closest relative through Naomi, and in accordance with Levirate law should be the next to marry her. Announcing herself, she entreats him to spread his cloak over her; he complies with this symbolic gesture of intention to marry her. Boaz marries Ruth, who gives birth to their son, Obed. Naomi now has a grandchild. Obed will become the grandfather of David and in that line, an ancestor of Jesus. As the story ends, the elders and the community offer this blessing for Boaz: "May the LORD make the woman who is coming into your house like Rachel and Leah, who together built up the house of Israel," adding, "may your house be like the house of Perez, whom Tamar bore to Judah" (4:11, 12). In this benediction, the people envision Ruth's full acceptance into the community of Israel along with the matriarchs Rachel and Leah and outsiders like Tamar.

The story of Ruth is read on multiple levels. It is a source of inspiration for women (and their families) who have had to flee their homeland because of war as in Syria, famine as in Somalia, or violence from cartels as in Guatemala, El Salvador, and Mexico. It is a model of successful assimilation and intermarriage between those from different ethnic and socio-economic backgrounds. Ruth's labor as a gleaner in a foreign land recalls the struggle of migrant workers seeking seasonal employment and immigrants who often face hostility and intolerance.

As a youth John recalls the flatbed trucks crowded with migrants who would arrive in southern Indiana for the tomato harvest. They were sheltered in drab cinder block rooms on a compound with limited amenities. The attacks on Asian Americans in recent years are also a sad commentary on the corrosion of appreciation for diversity within segments of society.

Florence recalls going to public school with the children of migrant workers who came to New York to pick beans. They disappeared just a few weeks after school began. She remembers her teachers carefully saving the workbooks of those children for when they returned in the late spring. How unsettling it must have been to keep adjusting to the multitude of classrooms in their itinerant lives!

On one level Ruth's story supports female dependence on men for survival and wellbeing and emphasizes the necessity for those men to take conscientious care of the women in their lives. On another level it features bold and outspoken women who take initiative and exercise power. This story, like that of Tamar, shows that without the cooperation of foreign-born women, the patrilineal genealogy of Jesus would be very different. Also, even though Ruth's story ends positively, as one commentator reminds us, "this is not the case for many poor women today, thousands of years later, whose stories often end quite tragically."[44]

The King and Another Man's Wife

The fourth unconventional woman in Matthew's genealogy of Jesus is identified only by her marital state, namely as "the wife of Uriah," though we know from 2 Samuel 11:3 she was Bathsheba. Her story begins with David on the roof of his royal house, gazing down at "a woman bathing; the woman was very beautiful" (2 Samuel 11:2). Even though he discovers that she was Uriah's wife, David has sex with her and she becomes pregnant. The narrator provides no insight into Bathsheba's character or her emotional response to her compromised relationship. Whether David and his lover were co-conspirators in this affair we are not told. Was Bathsheba an innocent victim of a powerful king or a willing partner who relished the opportunity for social advancement—or somewhere in the middle?

Entrapped with the visible result of an adulterous affair, David strategizes to exonerate himself by recalling Uriah the Hittite from the fighting and allowing him to visit his home, where he will presumably have relations with his wife. When this plot fails, David sends the Hittite warrior to the front with the heaviest fighting, where Uriah is killed. Then David marries Bathsheba and claims their son.

In today's culture, many may assume, based on stereotypes, that all men are susceptible to cheating. Does this imply that men have greater sexual needs? Surprisingly, studies show that women are unfaithful at about the same rate as men for reasons ranging from loneliness to boredom to unfulfilled emotional needs. Open marriages and open relationships are on the rise; and up to five percent of the population participate in consensual non-monogamy. Obviously, such practices are contrary to the teaching of Jesus (Mark 10:2–12).

David's misdeed does not escape the Lord, who sends Nathan the prophet to confront David with a pointed parable about a rich man and a poor man; the former steals the "one little ewe lamb" of the latter and prepares it to serve to a guest (12:1–15). David's "righteous" anger flares at this obvious injustice and he pronounces the death penalty for the aggressor: "the man who has done this deserves to die." Nathan must have stunned David with the rejoinder: "You are the man!" David had done what was evil in the Lord's sight and the punishment was severe. While the Lord spares David's life, the penalty was the death of the child that Bathsheba bore. And so it happened. David's pleas and fasting do not change the outcome.

Bathsheba and David have another son, whom they name Solomon. The Lord loves this heir to the throne (12:24), who becomes famous for his wisdom and the magnificent Temple he built in Jerusalem. When Solomon is on the throne, Bathsheba requests that he give his brother Adonijah the wife he wanted. Threatened, Solomon refuses and orders this rival to the throne killed. Bathsheba's power as queen mother apparently had its limits. Scholars have multiple theories explaining why she is not mentioned by name in Matthew's genealogy. Regardless of Matthew's reason, there is no doubt that this woman played a key role in the continuation of Jesus' royal ancestors, because she was the mother of Solomon, David's most prominent son.

The four women we have met here and the men around them demonstrate remarkable skill and assertiveness balanced with a touch of submission as they navigate the circumstances of their lives. The dynamics in these cases are not unlike those in very different cultural contexts, including what may be observed today in male/female interactions. As ancestors of Jesus, these four women also stand out as amazing examples of how God uses "the human sinful mess" to advance God's kingdom. The more one reads biblical narratives such as the stories of these four women, the more one realizes that God indeed writes the human story with crooked lines.

A Banquet, a Dance, and a Murder

Numerous people mentioned in the New Testament are part of the huge Herodian family that began with Herod the Great (72–4 BC). We will comment on two sets of these people: first the couple Herod Antipas and Herodias along with her daughter Salome, and then Agrippa II and Bernice, a brother and sister.

Herod Antipas, a son of Herod the Great, will simply be noted as Antipas here. He and his second wife Herodias (also a descendant of Herod the Great) were the rulers who had John the Baptist beheaded, with the help of her daughter (his stepdaughter) Salome. Mark, followed by Matthew, gives us the most scriptural details about this trio, although here and there Matthew actually corrected Mark's text. The Jewish historian Josephus tells us still more, such as Salome's name and the name of the fortress—Machaerus—where John was executed.

The Baptist's life is in jeopardy because he criticized the legality of the marriage between Antipas and Herodias. Herodias had previously been married to Antipas's brother and from this first union her daughter, Salome, was born. John's charge was that Antipas and Herodias violated the law of Levirate marriage, which we discussed in regard to Tamar and Ruth. Here, however, John's point was that Herodias *had* given birth to Antipas's brother's child, and hence she could *not* lawfully marry Antipas. It was considered incest because, unlike many people's contemporary understanding of incest, Herodias's first marriage had already made her a *blood* relative of her first husband's family. The Baptist had spoken the truth about this marriage, and Herodias is determined to eliminate him. She comes up with an ingenious way to do this. At a banquet, Salome performs what may have been an erotic dance that so affected the—likely inebriated—king that he promises her up to half his kingdom. Prompted by her vindictive mother's wish, Salome requests instead "the head of John the Baptist on a platter" (Mark 6:25).

Two biblical women once again seize power, this time during Herod's birthday banquet. Through intrigue and quick thinking they take control of unfolding events. Antipas is trapped due to the bold promise he had made in front of his courtiers. Salome and Herodias gamble on public pressure, getting their wish for John's head, aware that Antipas would be unwilling to back down in front of political friends. The women's scheme works! Through the centuries, authors, artists, and opera composers have probed Herodias's and Salome's motives for the intense hatred that prompted them to demand John's head on a platter. How could a scruffy prophet crying aloud in the desert have been so threatening? Perhaps the answer is obvious: those who speak truth to power, as did John and his cousin Jesus, wield an immense, but threatening, power themselves. The response, as in both their cases, is so often brutal execution.

A Shaken Monarch and His Sister

Agrippa II and Bernice, a Herodian brother/sister pair, are also interesting to bring out of the shadows. They were great-grandchildren of Herod the Great by his wife Mariamne I, the grandchildren of her son Aristobulus, and the children of his son Agrippa I. Agrippa II and Bernice appear in the Acts of the Apostles (25:13—26:32), where Luke writes at length about Paul's trial before the Roman governor Festus and then about his session with the Herodian siblings.[45]

As Luke describes the scene, the two Herodians enter the audience hall "with great pomp" and Festus brings Paul before them, explaining that he found nothing to condemn in Paul but also had no particular reason to grant his legal request to be remanded to Rome and the emperor for a further trial. Festus seeks especially Agrippa's input. In a lengthy defensive speech (no doubt with skillful editing by Luke), Paul appears to have shaken the king, who bluntly asks Paul, "Are you so quickly persuading me to become a Christian?" (Acts 26:28). As Festus, Agrippa, and Bernice exit the hall, they agree that Paul deserves neither death nor imprisonment.

At this trial, which can be dated to about AD 60, Bernice plays a minor role as Agrippa's consort (there were rumors, however, that they were an incestuous couple). In subsequent years during the disastrous war between the Jews and Rome (AD 66–70), Bernice emerged as an important player with the Roman military, even to the point of becoming the mistress of the Roman general Titus. After the Jews' defeat, and in the ensuing years when Titus eventually became emperor, Bernice followed him to Rome, expecting to marry him and serve as empress of the empire.

Titus indeed seemed to love her but was forced by the Senate to send her away; the Senate held that an emperor could not marry a non-Roman from the provinces. Unlike so many of the women we have discussed, Bernice had no tricks to employ at this point. Not only did Titus banish her to oblivion, but later historians have also failed to recognize her significance. She was moving in the same Roman circles as Josephus as he wrote his masterworks of history. She was undoubtedly one of his major sources on the Herodians. He never says so, but then, she was a woman.

The various personalities we have discussed here are in the shadows of the main events to many readers of the Bible. Their lives, however, add to the amazingly variegated chorus of men and women in the biblical texts. As we have seen before, their stories demonstrate how God picks up the pieces of fallible humans' moral choices that are often less than stellar. We hope you have enjoyed "meeting" these people! Let's move to our next chapter where we explore the person of Jesus, who had his own interactions with women and men from diverse backgrounds, both those on the margins and those in positions of power.

For Reflection:

- What are your thoughts about the inclusion of four women with colorful backgrounds in the genealogy of Jesus?
- What other minor biblical people have attracted your attention? Why do they stand out for you?

Chapter Six

This Tremendous Lover and Those Who Knew Him

He lived the life of a laborer in a small hamlet on the far reaches of the most dominant empire of his day. Born in humble circumstances to a provincial peasant woman and her husband, his life was mostly obscure until its last few years, when he touched others in a way that no one else had ever done before. His life did not end well. In fact it ended very badly. Though innocent of all charges, he suffered a violent, shameful death between two criminals. It was said that he died for the ungodly. The skeptic might ask: What honor is there in this? Yet his death was not the end of the story, as untold numbers throughout the centuries around the globe would attest. His name, of course, is Jesus of Nazareth.

> *Many years ago John was inspired by the remarkable spiritual classic* This Tremendous Lover *written by the Irish priest and Trappist Dom Mary Eugene Boylan. This book is about God's love story with humankind, summed up in what God has accomplished in the person of Jesus.*[46]

There is still much debate about how to characterize the man Jesus: Was he primarily an apocalyptic figure, wisdom teacher, miracle worker, kingdom preacher, a revolutionary, etc.? Apart from those debates these characteristics stand out in the Gospel portraits of him: He was a Galilean Jew, a designation that marks the land where he lived and the religious tradition he practiced. His magnetism and sense of authority drew people from all walks of life to come and see, to listen and engage, and ultimately to follow him. He was a skilled speaker whose parables drew on ordinary life experiences with astonishing lessons. He was approachable by those who lived on the margins—women and children, the wounded and ill, and the outcasts. A person of inner strength and courage, he did not back away from challenging the power brokers, both political and religious, calling them to account for their oppressive behaviors and their views of the Divine that were more restrictive than expansive. Jesus' life was all about being in tune with the presence of God and the mission he was called to fulfill.

In this chapter we'll explore central themes from the life of Jesus and highlight some of the men and women with whom he interacted. Join us in taking a fresh look at how Paul and the Gospel writers present Jesus with attention to his humanity. From Paul, our earliest source about Jesus, we learn certain important facts, namely that Jesus was "born of a woman," had a "brother" named James (Galatians 4:4, 1:19), and celebrated a memorial meal on the night of his betrayal (1 Corinthians 11:23–26). Paul also refers to the Christ (Jesus) who was crucified, died, and was buried (1 Corinthians 2:2, 15:3–4). Above all, Paul emphasizes the theological belief that God raised

Jesus from the dead, the "first fruits" of all who believe in him (1 Corinthians 15:20ff).

Most of what we know about Jesus comes from the Gospels. (Note that our intention is to focus on the Gospel portraits, not the historical Jesus.) The narrative of Jesus' public life begins with the evangelists' report that he encountered a man named John along the Jordan River who baptized him. During this event Jesus had a profound personal experience of God who claimed him as his Son. Scholars suggest that the Baptizer may have been Jesus' mentor, and that Jesus was initially a follower of John. What attracted Jesus to John and what did he hope to learn from this man in the wilderness? Was it his bold preaching? A desire for a rite of passage? Was it to discover his own unique purpose in life? Maybe it was all the above.

Immediately after his baptism, Jesus began to speak about the dawn of God's reign, but he described an event very unlike what his compatriots had been longing for, namely, a warrior leader who would overthrow their occupying oppressors, the Romans. Instead, the kingdom of God that Jesus described was about a new way of living, one marked by justice, love, and peace.

Teaching with Authority and Proclaiming Peace

Jesus embodied but also recast the ideals of masculinity from the dominant culture. These ideals included the ability to influence others, to exercise self-control, and to be a persuasive speaker. Jesus astounded others with his teaching and authority: "We have never seen anything like this!" (Mark 1:22, 2:12).

Are men and women both called to teach as Jesus did? It is unfortunate that the non-normative, culturally conditioned statement in First Timothy that calls for silencing women and prohibiting them from teaching or having authority over men has been used as a scriptural weapon to restrict women from exercising their gift as teachers (2:8–15), as Paul clearly articulates they can be in First Corinthians (12:28–31). In creating the new ministry of catechist in May 2021, Pope Francis affirmed that every catechist, man or woman, "must be a witness to the faith, a teacher and mystagogue, . . . who teaches for the Church."[47]

> *John recalls a Catholic parish where the pastor invited a woman who was a gifted speaker to offer a reflection on the Scriptures for a particular Sunday. Although a few parishioners were adamantly against having a woman in the pulpit, they were so inspired by her message that they later told the pastor. "You can invite her anytime to preach."*

In his message for the World Day of Peace (1995), St. John Paul II called on women in particular to be "teachers of peace with their whole being and in all their actions."[48] Dorothy Day was a Catholic pacifist who consistently spoke against all war. The recognition that Jesus extends to peacemakers in his revolutionary Sermon on the Mount is profound. He declares: "Blessed are the peacemakers, for they will be called children of God" (Matthew 5:9). This proclamation, along with the other Beatitudes, sets a new standard for masculinity and femininity that differs radically from Greco-Roman ideals where war and oppression were the means to bring "peace" in the empire. (Whether Jesus was a strict pacifist remains a debated question.)

Contrary to what the dominant image of masculinity may demand, Jesus does not declare blessed those who seek to control others, nor does he submit passively to oppression. Rather, he calls blessed the poor in spirit, the mourners, the meek, those who hunger for righteousness, the merciful, and the pure in heart. These are the perspectives that he offers for those striving to realize an authentic femininity or masculinity.

As we write in spring 2021, we are acutely aware that true and lasting peace has eluded tens of thousands around the globe. For years war has brought devastation to many countries including Afghanistan and Iraq, Lebanon and Syria, Guatemala and Somalia, to name a few. Unfortunately, in each of these conflicts mainly men have instigated and escalated the conflicts; mainly men have done the killing. Recently the United States has itself been called a war zone because of the plague of mass shootings, the shooting of minority group members by law enforcement, and the brutal hate attacks on Asian Americans. A staggering 98% of mass shootings have been committed by men. Does this data imply that men are more violent than women? Do both sexes have general feelings of aggression, but culture and society have so shaped behaviors that men commit more physically violent acts and women express aggression more indirectly, for example, by spreading rumors? Studies continue to focus on these questions.

One of Jesus' disciples resorted to violence when he drew a sword and cut off the right ear of the high priest's slave during Jesus' arrest. Jesus quelled this temptation to violence with the curt command "No more of this!" (Luke 22:50–51) in one Gospel, and a proverb, "all who take the sword will perish by the sword" (Matthew 26:51–52), in another.

Those living during the reign of the Roman Emperor Augustus experienced relative peace, captured by the slogan "*Pax Romana*" (Latin for "Peace of Rome"). However, this "peace" was achieved through brutal repression and maintained by cracking down on any hint of insurrection. Much more than the absence of war, the peace that Jesus brought echoed the Hebrew *Shalom*; it is a peace manifested by wholeness and harmony with oneself, one's neighbor, and one's God. The prophet Micah states this beautifully: what the Lord requires of us is "to do justice, and to love kindness, / and to walk humbly with your God" (Micah 6:8).

Face to Face with the Opposition

Almost from the get-go Jesus tangled with opponents, lots of them—all men. His expanding influence threatened the status of some authority figures and religious leaders among the people. Viewed from the perspective of sex, diminishment in the eyes of the crowd was a threat to their masculinity because it threatened their control. Jesus' own strategy was not motivated by attracting more followers and thus material influence, but rather by the higher mission entrusted to him by the Divine. His life was not about garnering public recognition; it was about doing God's will.

Jesus expressed his masculinity by outwitting his opponents (for example, Mark 2:23–28, 3:1–6, 7:1–13, 12:13–17). His language was colorful, even insulting. He compared some Pharisees to "whitewashed tombs": beautiful to look at on the outside, but full of dead bones and filth inside (Matthew 23:27). On the political front, he stood up to corrupt authorities—a demonstration of manhood—labeling Herod, who wanted to kill him, "that fox" (Luke 13:32; see chapter 4 above). He testified to Pilate that the true nature of his kingdom is "not from this world" and instructed this Roman procurator that "Everyone who belongs to the truth listens to my voice" (John 18:36, 37). In speaking truth to power, Jesus controlled the conversation. Although he was alone in this particular confrontation with an oppressive ruler, for most of his mission Jesus had a following of women and men whom he called to participate in his mission. He was not a lone ranger.

The Disciples: Eagerness, Failure, and Rehabilitation

In several ways Jesus was an unconventional male who invited others—largely, though not exclusively, men—to share in his way of life. In response, ordinary laborers, fishermen, and even a tax collector surprisingly abandoned their occupations and set off after Jesus. Disrupting social relations and responsibilities, Jesus called male providers to leave their wives and families. Maintaining family ties and fulfilling material obligations were not his top priorities. His hyperbolic statement: "Whoever comes to me and does not hate father and mother, wife and children, brothers and sisters . . . cannot be my disciple" is shocking (Luke 14:26). Because of such radical demands, it is no wonder that his own family tried to restrain him, for people thought he had "gone out of his mind" (Mark 3:21, see chapter 2 above). But Jesus did not mean that his followers should hold no affection or concern for family members. In fact, he criticized some Pharisees for encouraging people to give all that they have to God as an offering when doing so prevents them from taking care of their parents. Rather, Jesus' statement showed that his followers must place him first in their hearts and minds.

Reflecting the symbolism of the twelve tribes of Israel, Jesus called a motley band of twelve apostles. The fallible and contentious natures of these men are striking. They struggled to grasp the meaning of his parables (Mark 4:10, 13), argued over who was the "top dog" among them (Mark 9:33–35), and tried to prevent children from approaching him (Mark 10:13–16). Some might wonder whether these are indicators of what today is called male fragility—needing to establish and assert one's own knowledge and position.

The self-assertive Peter got it right when he responded to Jesus' query: "Who do you say that I am?" with the reply: "You are the Messiah" (Matthew 16:15, 16). However, this impetuous apostle utterly failed to comprehend that this very Messiah would also undergo great suffering, be rejected, and put to death. Totally exasperated, Jesus sternly reprimanded Peter: "Get behind me, Satan!" (Mark 8:32, 33). Nonetheless, Jesus never gave up on him or the other apostles. He appointed Peter as the rock of the church—the same person who would deny him (Matthew 26::69-75)—and promised that those who followed Jesus would sit "on twelve thrones, judging the twelve tribes of Israel" (Matthew 16:18, 19:28).

Related to this is the privileged role of three of the disciples, Peter, James, and John, whom Jesus invited to join him on a high mountain where "he was transfigured before them, and his clothes became dazzling white" (Mark 9:2–8). The disciples saw Moses and Elijah conversing with Jesus and the transfiguration of Jesus. At Jesus' instruction they kept this matter to themselves yet failed to grasp its meaning. The failure to understand the true mission of Jesus became apparent during Jesus' last days. During this fateful time, one of the Twelve denied knowing him, another betrayed him, and only one had the courage to be there when he hung dying on the cross. Just before his arrest, Jesus had warned that they would "all become deserters" and so they did (Mark 14:27). In so many instances the male disciples failed to embody the masculine qualities of strength and perseverance.

Yet it was these men to whom he entrusted his mission, and to whom after his death he extended his peace. Strengthened by the Spirit at Pentecost, they became fearless bearers of Jesus' message. Men's groups today who gather for support and friendship, for spiritual connection, for opportunities to explore their vulnerabilities and stressors, may find much encouragement by looking to the struggles and growth of the apostles. Their courageous activity is narrated in the Acts of the Apostles. It is unknown whether the man Jesus had any awareness of the profound effect his life and teaching would have on them after his death. The risen Christ, of course, lived among them and empowered them to witness valiantly to the power of God. Not only men, but women also received the Spirit. Several modern artists, in contrast to Leonardo da Vinci and his portrayal of the Last Supper, assume that of course women were present at large festive gatherings; their paintings include women along with men at the Last Supper and the Pentecost event (see Acts 1:14; 2:4, 17). We now turn to the human Jesus and his interactions with women.

The Women: Companions and Apostles

Though mentioned far less frequently, women played essential roles in the life of Jesus. Along with the Twelve, a group of many women accompanied Jesus as he traveled "through cities and villages, proclaiming and bringing the good news of the kingdom of God." Besides this, the women "provided for them [Jesus and his followers] out of their resources" (Luke 8:1–3). These women of means included Mary Magdalene, Joanna, and Susanna, along with "many others." They supported Jesus and the Twelve from their own financial resources. Beyond what we might imagine, these women helped Jesus understand the plight of ordinary women, like the woman who could not afford to lose even one silver coin (Luke 15:8–10), the bridesmaids who anxiously awaited the arrival of the bridegroom (Matthew 25:1–13), and the poor widow who contributed more than all the others to the Temple treasury (Mark 12:41–44).

Among those who supported Jesus was Mary Magdalene, not to be confused with the nameless woman, identified as "a sinner" (usually understood as a prostitute), who lavishly anointed the feet of Jesus while he dined at the house of a Pharisee (Luke 7:36–50). The wildly successful musical *Jesus Christ Superstar* portrays Mary Magdalene as a sexual temptress in love with Jesus, a supposed relationship passionately expressed in her theme song, "I Don't Know How to Love Him." The historical novel *The Last Temptation of Christ* (1955) by Nikos Kazantzakis and the bestseller *The Da Vinci Code* (2003) by Dan Brown go further: The former casts the Magdalene as betrothed to Jesus and the latter as Jesus' wife and mother of his children. There is no biblical basis for any of these sensational claims.

Surely Jesus had conversations with Mary Magdalene, but none of them are recorded in the Gospels. Her devotion to Jesus is indicated by her presence at the crucifixion, her witness to his burial in the tomb, and her participation in anointing his body (Mark 15:40, 47; 16:1). The most well-known, though often overlooked, role she played was that of "Apostle of the Resurrection," a title given to her by Thomas Aquinas. In the New Testament an apostle is a person sent by Jesus to bring an important message. Mary Magdalene, Joanna, and Mary the mother of James are the ones who brought the good news to the distraught male apostles that Jesus had risen. However, reflecting the limitations of their patriarchal perspectives, the men did not trust women's testimony. They dismissed the women's joyful announcement as "an idle tale" (Luke 24:10–11).

In the Fourth Gospel the risen Jesus calls Mary Magdalene by name, indicating his close relationship with her (John 20:16). There is some ambiguity about the way Jesus responded to Mary in their encounter. One translation reads: "Do not hold on to me" (verse 17, NRSV) and another: "Stop holding on to me" (NABRE). It is uncertain whether Mary intended to embrace Jesus or actually did embrace him. This moving personal scene has been referred to by the Latin expression *Noli me tangere* ("Do not touch me") and has been a favorite for painters to interpret. In June 2016 Pope Francis signed a decree elevating the celebration honoring Mary Magdalene from a memorial to a feast day in the liturgical calendar (July 22), placing her on a par with the male apostles whose festive name days are observed as feasts. Francis later referred to Mary Magdalene as an apostle of hope for the world. [49]

The Sisters in the Home: Docile Women or Engaged Leaders?

Jesus also had a close relationship with the sisters Martha and Mary (she was not Mary Magdalene), visiting their home more than once. While on his journey to Jerusalem, Jesus stopped by for what was probably a much-needed rest with close friends (Luke 10:38–42). Martha offered hospitality by welcoming him and Mary by attending to him, sitting at his feet listening and learning. Mary's pose is typical for male disciples who are attentive to their teacher. "Her place at Jesus' feet," one commentator reflects, "represents . . . the openhearted, self-giving love of the true disciple who wants to learn and to share that learning through teaching."[50]

Tension arises between the sisters; Martha, coping with all she has to do, is discontent because her sister is not helping. Jesus' response to Martha, "there is need of only one thing," is not dismissive, but rather a reframing, emphasizing the importance of attending to guests in general and, specifically, to Jesus' words. In calling her twice by name, "Martha, Martha," Jesus' approach is sympathetic, not judgmental. The learning for Martha is not about her activity of preparing food—which is indeed a real sign of hospitality—but rather her anxiousness. Based on an alternate manuscript tradition, Jesus' message to her may be to keep the preparation to a minimum and to join her sister Mary, learning at his feet.[51]

On the other hand, some feminists read the passage as Luke's effort to suppress traditions of active, prominent women in the Jesus movement, in preference for more passive, docile ones.[52] This perspective has bolstered the ideological stance that women are not to hold church leadership positions, whether ordained or otherwise. In the story does Martha's complaint to Jesus about not appreciating her household *diakonia* (Greek, "service," verse 40), imply, as some commentators suggest, that the Lukan Jesus would likewise not support female *diakonia* within the church? Was Martha, and hence the *diakonia* of women, really being squelched by Luke? These are questions not easily answered but of interest to those debating the re-institution of female deacons in the contemporary church such as occurred in the Synod on the Amazon (2019) and is currently a subject of interest in other synodal discussions.

The Fourth Gospel narrates a lengthy episode about Martha, Mary, and their brother Lazarus, all of whom, the evangelist comments, Jesus loved (John 11:1–44). The sisters request Jesus' presence, because their beloved brother is dying. Jesus waits until Lazarus has died to go to the family. Martha goes out of the village to receive Jesus and confronts him about his tardy response, thus holding him accountable for her brother's death. She engages in a theological conversation with Jesus, culminating in her dramatic profession of faith: "I believe that you are the Messiah, the Son of God, the one coming into the world" (11:27). Like Peter, who professed that Jesus is the Messiah in the synoptic Gospels, Martha solemnly proclaims faith in Jesus as the Christ. Since Peter is granted broad authority to bind and loose in Matthew's account, the reader may wonder what authority may have been conferred upon Martha for being the first to make this profession of faith in the Johannine community.

As John's narrative continues, Jesus goes to where Lazarus was buried and sees Mary and others weeping. Then "Jesus began to weep" (11:35). Often cited as the shortest verse in the New Testament, this brief comment exemplifies Jesus' heartfelt emotional response to the death of his friend. Contrary to the sentiment in the popular song "Big Boys Don't Cry," and the stereotypical expectation that real men don't shed tears, in a moment of male vulnerability Jesus gives free expression to the depth of his sadness at the loss of a friend.

Later in John's Gospel, Martha, Mary, and Lazarus hold a dinner party for Jesus, perhaps to celebrate Lazarus' restoration to life (12:1–8). While Jesus is in their home, Mary anoints his feet with costly perfume. Judas challenges the extravagant waste, but Jesus defends Mary's action, interpreting this as an anticipation of his burial. Mary's ritual "washing" foreshadows Jesus' washing the feet of the disciples (John 13:1–20). Her loving act of service parallels what Jesus will teach the disciples, saying to them: "I have set you an example, that you also should do as I have done to you." Mary demonstrates true faith, and thus becomes an "authentic model of discipleship."[53] For her part, Martha's protest to Jesus about his delay in their prior encounter brings to mind other instances when women challenged Jesus, for example, his mother at the wedding feast of Cana (chapter 2, above). We now explore the confrontation between Jesus and the Syrophoenician woman.

A Determined Woman Challenges the Jewish Teacher

During his travels Jesus makes one of his rare excursions into Gentile territory (Mark 7:24–30). He planned to enter a house undetected, but a woman with a daughter who needed healing hears about his presence and shows up uninvited. Bowing down at his feet she begs him to expel the demon which she thought caused the illness. Jesus responds sharply: "Let the children be fed first, for it is not fair to take the children's food and throw it to the dogs" (Mark 7:27). Dogs, as unclean and irrational animals, is a derogatory term used by Jesus to refer to Gentiles, and by implication to this woman who is a Gentile.

Refusing to be easily dismissed, the desperate mother, who dares to transgress divisive norms, offers Jesus a lesson of her own: "Sir, even the dogs under the table eat the children's crumbs" (7:28). She accepts the comparison of her people to dogs, but, outwitting Jesus, argues that even they deserve to be fed. In answering back to Jesus, she crosses social boundaries; it was expected that men called the shots and had the last say while women were to be silent and submissive.

Because of her retort, the woman gets her way. Exercising her agency, she succeeds in persuading Jesus to change his mind. Jesus, acknowledging her perspective, yields to her request: "For saying that, you may go—the demon has left your daughter." Remarkably, this woman is the only person in the synoptic Gospels who comes out ahead in a dispute with Jesus. Not only that, after Jesus' reversal in this exchange he "changes his strategy" and "travels through gentile lands, where he heals and feeds people (Mark 7:31—8:9)."[54] While this woman shows respect for Jesus, nothing is said about her faith in Mark's account (compare Matthew 15:21-28).

This passage has implications for the contemporary church on multiple levels. The text reflects structural inequality between those who have a place at the table and those who do not. Belonging to the latter, this Syrophoenician woman, begging for food and recognition, is among the marginalized. In this respect, Pope Francis has emphasized that the "The Gospel of the Marginalized Is Where Our Credibility Is Found and Revealed" (homily July 15, 2015, St. Peter's Basilica). This text is about hearing the voices of those on the margin as Jesus did in response to this empowered woman.

Men of Status Respond in Faith to Jesus

There are also some men whose interactions with Jesus are significant. We will briefly bring into the limelight four men with social rank who respond positively to Jesus. One is a leading Jew, another is a chief tax collector, and two are Roman centurions. The leading Jew is Nicodemus, a Pharisee who was a member of the ruling class. (The Pharisees were a devout lay reform movement within Judaism, and Jesus' criticisms target only those who were duplicitous.) He approaches Jesus under cover of darkness, not so much out of fear, but to avoid attention (John 3:1–21). He recognizes Jesus as "a teacher who has come from God." Jesus instructs him about needing to be born again, a phenomenon which Nicodemus finds literally incomprehensible. Still, he is receptive to Jesus and may have become a disciple. Later in the Gospel he defends Jesus, asserting his right to a hearing (7:51), and after Jesus' death he brings "a mixture of myrrh and aloes, weighing about a hundred pounds"—an extraordinary amount—to anoint the body of Jesus (19:39).

Zacchaeus was a rich tax collector who was curious about Jesus (Luke 19:1–10). He heard that Jesus was passing through Jericho, and being short, he climbed a tree to be able to see the itinerant preacher. Noticing him, Jesus addressed him and invited himself (!) to Zacchaeus' house. Deeply moved, this rich man made the generous pledge to give half his possessions to the poor and to repay those he defrauded four times as much. Jesus then declares: "Today salvation has come to this house, because he too is a son of Abraham" (19:9). Jesus includes this man among his own people. No longer is he an outsider, as tax collectors—collaborators with the Roman oppressors—were considered to be.

A centurion, a Roman military commander at Capernaum, was concerned about one of his slaves, who was close to death (Luke 7:1–10). He sends Jewish elders, who reported to Jesus that "he loves our people, and . . .

built a synagogue for us." The centurion felt unworthy to have Jesus come to his home. While Jesus is on his way there, the centurion sends a messenger to request that Jesus simply "speak the word" so that his servant would be healed. Jesus acts and the healing takes place. Commending this centurion, Jesus tells the crowd, "Not even in Israel have I found such faith."

Another centurion is described at the scene of Jesus' crucifixion. His presence is no surprise. He was sent to maintain peace while the death penalty was carried out for the condemned criminals. But the centurion's response to what he sees is astounding. Facing Jesus and observing the way he breathed his last, the Roman commander professes: "Truly this man was God's Son!" (Mark 15:39). In our day, Sr. Helen Prejean, known for her bestselling book *Dead Man Walking* (1993), has devoted much of her ministry to accompanying those on death row, and to witnessing their executions, inhumane practices she seeks to abolish. Both in the time of the centurion and today, the final words of the dying and the experiences of those who witness their deaths—whether violent or not—often become insightful and memorable.

Four men of distinction; four positive responses to the man from Galilee: pondering the necessity of being born again, being included as a son of Abraham, having a remarkable faith. They were all transformed. These four men, along with so many others, women and men, came to know this tremendous lover, and as a result their lives were changed.

Breathing His Last on the Cross

The Greeks and the Romans highly esteemed the male body. Their surviving nude statues in marble attest to how much they revered the human form, particularly that of males. In his last days Jesus' body was subjected by Roman soldiers to a level of violent disfigurement that is hard to comprehend. Mel Gibson's *The Passion of the Christ* (2004) dramatizes Jesus' suffering in a way that leaves little to the imagination. Crowned with thorns, his flesh torn with barbed whips, hands and feet shattered with piercing nails, and his side sliced open with a soldier's lance, the severely marred body of Jesus appeared very unmanly. An outsider might think that nothing of this man's masculinity remains.

However, other factors transform perceptions for those open to "see" in a different way. Reflecting features of a noble death, Jesus approached his last days voluntarily. Although Jesus was arrested and led away, the Fourth Evangelist portrays him as being in complete control of events, a supreme irony. What transformed the perception of Jesus' death from being a shameful defeat to a salvific victory was his resurrection. In this, God completely vindicated Jesus. Through the cross and resurrection, the dominant cultural motif of masculinity was turned on its head. God's action in these events radically re-defined masculinity and femininity as well. Those whose lives are guided by the will of God and fashioned by the Son, this tremendous lover, are the "real" men and "real" women.

For Reflection:

- What do you find most appealing about the way Jesus expressed his masculinity?
- What dimensions of being masculine today might Jesus challenge the most?

Chapter Seven

From the Amazon and Guatemala to Tarsus

Dorothy woke up on February 12, 2005, for an early morning walk to speak to community members about their land rights and the rainforests of the Amazon. Two armed men who worked for a livestock company followed her. When they asked about any weapons she was carrying, she replied that the Bible was her only weapon. Then she read to them a passage from the Beatitudes: "Blessed are the poor in spirit, for theirs is the kingdom of heaven" (Matthew 5:3). Taking a few more steps, one man called her "sister," and within moments the other man gunned her down, firing shots to her abdomen and head.

A member of the Sisters of Notre Dame de Namur, Dorothy Stang had dedicated almost forty years of her life to advocating for the poor in Brazil and defending the rainforest from devastation. She stood with the peasants at the mercy of the gangs and ranchers who wanted to confiscate their plots. She had the courage to speak out boldly on behalf of the persecuted and powerless.

Our friend Charlie, now around 80, has shared reflections about his work as a Maryknoll missionary among the indigenous people in Guatemala, a country ravaged by a well-equipped army supported by the U.S. government and the CIA. During the civil war that lasted more than thirty-five years, there were untold numbers of abuses in addition to the killing of 200,000 people, including many catechists, religious, priests, and bishops. Charlie lived and worked closely with Juan José Gerardi Conedera. Later named bishop, after the war Gerardi served on the National Reconciliation Commission. Their report, *Guatemala: Nunca más* (Never Again), made public in 1998, attributed most of the atrocities to the army. Two days after it was issued, Bishop Gerardi was bludgeoned to death in the garage of the parish house adjacent to San Sebastian Church.

During the time we ourselves spent in Guatemala, we stood in silence outside the place where Gerardi suffered a martyr's death. This fearless leader spoke out boldly in a cry for justice. Both he and Dorothy were following in the footsteps of an ancient man from Tarsus whose life was all about bold speaking. All three paid the ultimate price for such courage. Let's turn to his life now.

This man from Tarsus was cosmopolitan and controversial. He assembled coworkers and other collaborators. He tangled with agitators and troublemakers, with officials and kings. He professed to be all things to all people. Humble and boastful, weak and strong, he was a passionate preacher, a messenger of peace and grace. He is one of the most important men in the New Testament. His name is Paul, and his impact on Christianity has been no less than extraordinary.

A Well-Educated Man

Knowing where a person is from already tells us a great deal. Paul was a diaspora Jew born in the city of Tarsus in Asia Minor (modern Turkey). Luke described this urban center as "an important city" (Acts 21:39). In his Hellenistic environment, he received what we might consider a higher level education. There he would have been introduced to popular philosophers and the mystery cults, as well as Greek education and multiple aspects of Greek culture and religion. As a Jew, Paul had impeccable credentials. He was from the tribe of Benjamin, a Hebrew born of Hebrews; he was a zealous Pharisee, and blameless under the law (Philippians 3:5–6). The New Testament says almost nothing about his family, apart from one reference to a sister and her son (Acts 23:16). There is no consensus about whether Paul was ever married; if he had been this does not seem to be the case when he writes his letters.

Passionate about his Jewish beliefs, Paul tried to violently destroy "the church of God," because, to his mind, its members veered from his ancestral religion. All that changed when God revealed his Son to Paul and set him on a different course (Galatians 1:13–16), traveling throughout the eastern Mediterranean preaching the risen Christ among the Gentiles. Amid successes and failures, Paul dedicated the remainder of his life to founding communities of Christ believers. He wrote several pastoral letters offering encouragement and instruction, often addressing community problems that emerged.

In the previous chapter, we identified a number of qualities of ideal masculinity from Greco-Roman culture. Here we will consider the attributes of strength, physical appearance, rhetorical skills, and character. In his letter to the Philippians, Paul claims to be supremely strong: "I can do all things through him who strengthens me" (4:13). To Paul's contemporaries who did not believe in Jesus the Messiah, it was inconsequential whether one's strength was innate or derived from an external source. In Paul's own perception, he was, as a man, very strong.

Although not a warrior himself, Paul employed military metaphors that he co-opted from Roman military culture. The dominant and ubiquitous presence of the Roman army with its well-equipped soldiers provided a storehouse of images for him to draw upon to construct a warrior masculinity. Ironically the very instruments of war that threatened his fellow believers served to define life in Christ. This imagery reflected the male power and dominance of the world in which they lived. Paul urged believers of both sexes to fortify themselves for the day of the Lord by putting on "the breastplate of faith and love, and for a helmet the hope of salvation" (1 Thessalonians 5:8). Such imagery was particularly useful in his self-defense. Paul asserts that he and his collaborators "do not wage war according to human standards; for the weapons of our warfare are not merely human, but they have divine power to destroy strongholds. We destroy arguments . . . and we take every thought captive to obey Christ" (2 Corinthians 10:3–5).

Paul's masculinity came under a fierce attack in Corinth, as he relays in this letter. He quotes charges against him by opponents he dubbed "super-apostles" (11:5): "For they say, 'His letters are weighty and strong, but his bodily presence is weak, and his speech contemptible'" (10:10). Robust physical appearance and bodily integrity were important characteristics of manhood. When Paul recounts his imprisonments along with "countless floggings" by Roman and Jewish authorities (11:23) he implies a rejection of "certain traditional standards of masculinity."[55] Against the charge that his personal presence was ineffective, Paul firmly rejects the cultural assumption that masculinity is demonstrated by outward appearance, domination, or power. He appeals to the Corinthians rather on the basis of "the meekness and gentleness of Christ" (10:1). Far from being apologetic, Paul claims his meekness and gentleness as a badge of honor.

As for Paul's speech being "contemptible," perhaps it was his forthrightness to which his listeners reacted. Paul understood himself to be a courageous speaker whose boldness (Greek *parrhesia*) was both a divine gift and a human characteristic, made possible by God, that he and his associates manifested (Colossians 2:15, 1 Thessalonians 2:2). Paul understood that he had the authority to exercise boldness not through any innate rhetorical ability but because he spoke "in/through God" and "in Christ." That he chose to not always exercise that authority is indicated in his letter to Philemon, verses 8–9.

While imprisoned, Paul presents himself as relying on the prayer of believers *so that* he may speak with boldness, implying that their spiritual support enabled him to speak as he must (Ephesians 6:19–20). In other words, one's own resources, even spiritual resources, are not sufficient to proclaim the gospel.

Paul's courage to speak out boldly occurs often in the face of fierce opposition (1 Thessalonians 2:2) or in adverse circumstances. This is not surprising, since courageous proclamation of the gospel does rouse up defiance from those who are closed off to the message. There are social and political consequences to being courageous in speech or action. Even the courage it took to publicly affirm one was a believer is a dimension of *parrhesia*.

A Host of Coworkers

Like Jesus, Paul worked closely with both female and male collaborators. Among the men were Barnabas, John Mark, and Silvanus. Most of Paul's letters include one or more co-senders, all male. These were Timothy, Silvanus, and Sosthenes. A host of women are mentioned by name in Paul's letters and Acts, most of whom are sadly not known to Christians today. Among them are Lois and Eunice, known for their faith. Others, such as Lydia, were the heads of households. Paul's coworkers included Euodia,

Syntyche, and Prisca. He also names one deacon, Phoebe, and one apostle, Junia.

Regarding Phoebe, there is a vibrant movement of the Spirit in the church today directed toward the discernment of women for the diaconate. With respect to Junia, for much of church history her name has been erroneously read as the male name Junias, on the mistaken assumption that there were no female apostles during the times of Jesus and Paul. In addition to these women, over a dozen others are mentioned by name, many of them in the recommendations and greetings in chapter 16 of Romans.

Paul's Perspective toward Women

In the biblical documents by and about Paul one encounters many women by name who collaborated with him in forming the earliest churches. The continually unfolding women's movement has brought intense scrutiny upon Paul and these Pauline women due to the limitation on women's leadership in Christian groups of many denominations. One rationale for why women were excluded from leadership rests upon the shallow argument that since women did not lead or preside in the earliest churches, women are not permitted to lead or preside now either. This type of argument—"they couldn't, so you can't"—incenses many biblical scholars who see in the texts the obvious presence of female leadership.

The evidence shows that women were active leaders in the early church. This is all the more remarkable since everything we know about them is contained within androcentric texts, notably by Paul and Luke. Furthermore, theologians have pointed out that no one is limited by what was done in the past. The churches themselves have developed dramatically! Christianity goes forward in history not in a static mode but in obedience to the power of the Holy Spirit.

Closer study of women in Paul's undisputed letters and in the Pastoral Letters (First and Second Timothy and Titus) brings to the forefront Paul's relationship with women. Many argue that the Pastorals, which contain strikingly negative statements about women, were not written by Paul and hence cannot be used to accuse him of being a misogynist. Far from being prejudiced against women, Paul worked along with them just as he did with men. He praised them as coworkers, never relating to them as inferiors. It appears to these scholars that it was the authors of the pastorals who intended to restrict women's roles and in a later time were writing in Paul's name to bolster their position.

Unexpected Paths for a Memorable Couple

Both Paul's male and female collaborators strike us as interesting persons in themselves. Let's zero in here on one married couple, the tent-makers Prisca and Aquila. They were

Paul's very close coworkers who hosted house churches successively in Corinth, Ephesus, and Rome. Aquila was Jewish and Prisca, most likely a Gentile, was possibly of an upper class (since none of the thousands of known Roman inscriptions about slaves use her name). It may be that from a Roman social perspective she had married "beneath her status." The couple had converted in Rome, it seems, but were soon expelled along with other Christ-believing Jews due to an imperial decree designed to quell disruptions in synagogues, probably over preaching about the Christ.

After fleeing from Rome, Prisca (also called Priscilla) and Aquila had supplied Paul with both work and lodging when they first met each other in Corinth. There this couple opened their home not only to Paul but also to other local believers. Paul speaks about "the church in their house" (1 Corinthians 16:19), which became, in the words of Pope Francis, a *domus ecclesiae*, "a place in which to listen to the Word of God and celebrate the Eucharist." Francis adds, "Even today, in some countries where there is no religious freedom and Christians have no freedom, Christians still meet in a house, a little hidden, to pray and celebrate the Eucharist."[56] Pope Francis makes an interesting point about the Word and the Eucharist being celebrated in the home of this lay couple. Scholars speculate as to who might have served as the leader of these worship experiences, because the text does not reveal this information.

From Corinth Paul, Prisca, and Aquila traveled to Ephesus. When Paul left to go to Jerusalem, they stayed to pastor their house church and remained active in synagogue disputes about Jesus. During that time an Alexandrian Jew named Apollos had stirred up debates in Ephesus through his enthusiastic preaching about Jesus. While he "taught accurately the things concerning Jesus," he "knew only the baptism of John." Luke reports that it was Prisca and Aquila who "took him aside and explained the Way of God to him more accurately" (Acts 18:25, 26).

This couple would later return to Rome and host a church in their house there as well. There is no indication that Paul ordered them around; their mutual respect was rooted in the mission to witness to the resurrection of the Lord and shepherd the groups of believers which formed around them. Some scholars think Prisca may have been the more dominant teacher or preacher of the two, since she is, unusually for the time, named first when the couple is mentioned. Due to her origins she may have also been the more literate. If so, did Prisca challenge contemporary patriarchal views of what a married woman's role should be? Was it acceptable for men to listen to her teach? Her involvement certainly was not threatening to Paul.

As persons of their day, Prisca and Aquila were well-travelled and knowledgeable about the religious developments that had touched their lives. They eventually returned to Rome, where Paul sent greetings to them in the Letter to the Romans. His message tells us a lot about them: "Greet Prisca and Aquila, who work with me in Christ Jesus, and who risked their necks for my life, to whom not only I give thanks, but also all the churches of the Gentiles. Greet also the church in their house" (Romans 16:3–5).

Probably it was during their prior years together in Ephesus that Prisca and Aquila had somehow rescued Paul. In First Corinthians he comments on this period and how he had "fought with wild animals" in Ephesus (15:32). We cannot be sure whether those were real beasts or beastly humans, nor how the couple rescued him.

We can only imagine their subsequent years back in Rome, during the 60s. Maybe Prisca and Aquila occasionally sat by the Tiber and mused, as many of us might, about the unexpected paths their lives had taken since they had become Christ-believers. If they did live into those years they would have been on hand to welcome Paul into the city as a prisoner. According to Lukan tradition (Acts 28:30), he was able to speak with "all who came to him" during his house arrest. Was Peter also there in those days, in this period when all Christians in Rome faced much danger? And did Prisca and Aquila live long enough to be caught up in the Neronian persecution? Were they themselves, as tradition holds about Paul and Peter, martyred? Were they among the believers thrown to wild animals in Nero's circus or burned on stakes as torches for the emperor's depraved games? If only we could ask them . . .

For travelers to Rome, the stones of many millennia of history lie beneath their feet and within the walls of buildings, remade of older buildings time and again. In a few places one can be rather sure Paul, Prisca, and Aquila trod across those same spaces. The area of the city named Trastevere ("across the Tiber") is known to have been the region where many Jews, and thus early Christians, lived during the era of Paul, Prisca, and Aquila. A bridge from their days still crosses from the city proper over to Trastevere. In such places, and so many other spots in Rome, we can walk with at least some certainty in their footsteps. It is a good thing to do. Stopping to reflect a moment while on "their bridge" helps a traveler remember those who poured their energy into preaching Christianity's good news—and the ones who lost their lives in doing so.

Some Roads Lead to Martyrdom

Paul, Prisca, and Aquila lived in an exciting and cosmopolitan, yet deadly, era. Paul for certain was martyred, and maybe Prisca and Aquila as well. They point our thoughts forward to today, to those who are also sincerely following their Christian, sometimes unexpected, paths and have already or may at any time be martyred. We would like to tell you about some people we met in a distant country whose very lives, even as we write now, may be in danger.

We went to Myanmar (formerly called Burma) in 2013. While visiting our daughter, Anne, who was there studying Burmese, we taught a course on Paul at a Catholic religious studies college in Yangon, the former capital. Our students were religious sisters and brothers of all ages, seminarians, and lay people from throughout the country. For Myanmar and its people those were the heady, hopeful days of the early opening of the country and increasing freedom under Aung San Suu Kyi. She had long been a leader for human rights even in the many years she was under house arrest; she was a Nobel Peace Prize winner (1991) and, as of our time there, and in an amazing election, she had become the State Counsellor (equivalent to Prime Minister). She had thus played a major role in Myanmar's transition from rule by a military junta to partial democracy beginning in the 2010s.

As we encountered Burmese students in 2013, the country was exciting, with new buildings everywhere, tourists coming in growing numbers, an economy improving rapidly, and a hopeful future. A movie entitled *The Lady* (2011), the Burmese nickname for Suu Kyi, captures the period well. Our approximately fifty students were filled with faith and hope as they continued their ministry in challenging circumstances. They shared with us their plans to improve and extend the Catholic educational network and the pastoral programs. They were eager to bring the spirit of Vatican II to a country that had been largely isolated for several decades. Catholics make up only 1 percent of Myanmar's population, which is primarily Buddhist with small percentages of other groups. As a small community, all the Catholics tend to know each other; they personally know their bishops and other religious leaders. In Yangon they frequently congregate at the large cathedral with their courageous archbishop, Cardinal Charles Maung Bo. Even the Vatican delegate making a formal visit to the region interacted with the local community members. For our students, the highlight of his trip was when he took the time to visit our classroom and engaged them in conversation.

The Thirteenth Station of the Cross

As we write this in April 2021, the political landscape of Myanmar has radically changed. A military junta again seized power, arresting Suu Kyi and other government leaders on February 1, 2021, after declaring the recent general election fraudulent. Her own diplomatic history is extremely complex and deeply tainted by her reluctance to speak out against the genocide of the Rohingya Muslim minority. As this book goes to press (late fall 2022), the junta continues its unrelenting oppression of the Catholic Church, destroying churches and murdering the faithful. Here we wish to focus on what has happened to our students in light of the recent junta takeover and the resulting oppression.

While the junta has closed off internet access for the most part, reports are that protests against the takeover have turned increasingly violent. One highly publicized photo shows Sister Ann Rose Nu Tawng in the city of Myitkyina kneeling in dust before armed police officers, garbed in her simple habit, just as many of our students were, and with outspread arms; she was begging them not to hurt children in the crowd. She explained later, "I knelt down . . . begging them not to shoot and torture the children, but to shoot me and kill me instead."[57] This image of Sister Ann shatters us because it could be a picture of many of our student sisters, some of whom are from that city . . . and tragically, not knowing what is ahead for the people of Myanmar, it may yet be. Even as we write, the junta is escalating its force and the protests are growing as well.

Cardinal Charles Bo has forcefully and boldly spoken out, reflecting the Pauline quality of *parrhesia* (discussed above). He travelled to Myitkyina a few days after eighty people were killed by heavy artillery fire in Bago. To his people he reflected: “For many of you, the thirteenth station of the Cross, of Our Mother crying over the dead body of her Son, became real. We live in a country where hundreds of mothers live with inconsolable tears and their hearts wounded, like our Mother Mary, with the sight of their sons and daughters tortured and killed.”[58] Both Cardinal Bo and Pope Francis have demanded an end to the bloodshed throughout the country. (As we edit this in August 2022, Aung San Suu Kyi is still jailed in solitary confinement; Catholic villages have been burned and individuals have been arrested and killed; Cardinal Bo continues to boldly speak out.)

Many modern believers, like our students in Myanmar and elsewhere around the world, are facing dangers they may never have predicted. They echo the times of Paul, Prisca, and Aquila, who could hardly have foreseen how their lives in Rome would turn out, although they undoubtedly sensed the growing animosity toward Christians. What might Paul tell us? Once, in reflecting on the future, he wrote: “This one thing I do: forgetting what lies behind, and straining forward to what lies ahead, I press on toward the goal for the prize of the heavenly call of God in Christ Jesus” (Philippians 3:13–14).

For Reflection:

- Has being a Christian led you to take paths you never expected to follow?
- If you are not aware of the places and ways in which Christian brothers and sisters around the world are endangered because of their faith, look up several of these situations. How do the dangers these Christians face in holding and practicing their beliefs affect your own faith?

Chapter Eight

Outliers No More

Among the outliers in the church today are women like Ashley, who became a single mother because her husband died. She said, regarding parish life, "I felt on the outside looking in at the time, without anybody being deliberately rude." Another single mother felt "branded with a scarlet letter."[59] Outliers also include divorced and remarried Catholics. In society, outliers encompass a wide range of people such as Asian Americans, African Americans, Native Americans, and undocumented workers. The Bible recounts several stories where circumstances put women and men on the outside. They risked or experienced exclusion and marginalization from the community. In this chapter we discuss some of these biblical individuals and the challenges they faced. Their stories bring to mind those today who may feel marginalized, on the outside looking in, hoping for understanding, recognition, and validation.

We begin with Hannah and women like her who face the challenge of infertility. At least for a time, their lives seem to fail to fulfill God's great commandment to humankind: "Be fruitful and multiply" (Genesis 1:28). Two of the women without children are the banished foreign queen Vashti and Esther, a Jewish woman who replaces her. Esther becomes queen in a foreign land and from that position plays a key role in saving her people from destruction.

Other outliers are two couples, Job and his wife and Hosea and his wife Gomer. On the narrative level, these husbands and wives really struggle in coming to terms with difficult situations. The former pair are afflicted with a crescendo of losses that would crush the hearts of even the most steadfast. The tale of Hosea and Gomer takes us inside a story, whether real or allegorical, where God's prophet is asked to take a prostitute as his wife. The last two characters we will consider are Gentiles who encounter the two leading apostles of the early church: The centurion Cornelius has a dream that puts him into contact with Peter, and the businesswoman Lydia becomes the host to Paul. The lives of all four are changed by these encounters.

Barren Hannah and Those Desiring Motherhood

One rarely hears the word "barrenness" today outside of biblical studies. Instead, the related medical term "infertility" is commonly used to name the painful reality of those who are unable, at least for a period of time or ever, to bear children.

The stories of barrenness in the Bible include women such as Sarah, Hannah, and Elizabeth. Here we will consider Hannah's story (1 Samuel 1:1—2:10), a tale situated in the hill country of Ephraim. Hannah was the wife of

Elkanah, whose other wife, Peninnah, had given birth to many children. Every year when Elkanah took his two wives with him to the shrine at Shiloh, Peninnah would taunt Hannah severely "to irritate her, because the LORD had closed her womb" (1:6). Finally, in deep distress Hannah made a vow to the Lord which Eli, the priest of the shrine, overheard. She promised that if God gave her a son she would raise him as a nazirite, a vowed individual who followed ascetic practices for a period (1:9–11). Eli reassured her that the Lord would grant her prayer (1:17). After giving birth to Samuel, Hannah kept her promise. He became the last of the judges and a great prophet. Hannah bore five more children.

Are stories like Hannah's comforting to infertile couples today? To make a vow to God, which God then answers positively, seems like a straightforward way to get help from God. It's like making a deal. Probably a huge majority of people have tried it regarding some profound help they need. But does success in "dealing" with God match up with most human experience? Does God seem to answer our deepest prayers made with a bargaining plea, not just regarding infertility but on a whole range of concerns? For every Hannah, how many other infertile women and men have prayed for a child without feeling any answer to their prayers?

Human deals are ways we attempt to control God and our own destinies. But Jesus himself taught us about trying to influence God as he prayed in the Garden of Gethsemane: "Father, if you are willing, remove this cup from me; yet, not my will but yours be done" (Luke 22:42). Should we not pray likewise? Jesus' lament in crying out to God in human pain gives us permission to do the same when we ourselves are in distress. We are left then to wait upon God. Spiritual literature is filled with stories of people who felt their prayers were eventually answered but often in ways they never imagined. Frequently this is only recognized in retrospect.

So, do biblical stories about God granting children to barren women help infertile women and couples today? Occasionally, barren women take matters into their own hands. In Hannah's case she thought making a vow might help—and to her it seemed to do so. Sarah dealt with her infertility by telling Abraham to have a child by Hagar, only to be surprised by her own later conception of Isaac. In our times, of course, praying as Jesus did remains a believer's deepest expression of hope. And medical science thankfully has more and more options couples can pursue, especially since infertility is a medical condition for growing numbers.

For some, infertility is medically permanent, giving them no hope for bearing a child. Still, the barren women of the Bible may speak to them in surprising ways. There are a multitude of women throughout the whole Bible who accomplished amazing things yet were not defined by motherhood. Kaya Oakes comments that "women who live without children adapt and survive," adding:

> "This is what Esther, Miriam, Vashti, Judith, . . . Anna the prophetess, Mary and Martha of Bethany, and many of the women in the early church like Lydia, Junia and Phoebe—none of whom are described as mothers—had to do to survive in their own era. Any woman trying to recreate herself when others have looked at her and seen only emptiness may instead find other ways to nurture and care for the world around her."[60]

Those sentiments are very inspiring and can help someone find a path forward, but at the same time no one should ever underestimate the pain caused by infertility.

A Banished Princess and a Beautiful Queen

A jarring example of the unequal treatment of women and men was reported in the news in 2020. A Saudi princess who was active in promoting women's rights in her country was detained, while the crown prince of the same country, who was widely believed to have engineered the murder of a journalist, remained free. This strikes us as not far removed from the biblical story of Esther.

In one of the few canonical books that is named after a woman, Esther is the protagonist of a fictional story about a deposed queen, and the woman who replaced her. This fictional narrative of surprising reversals begins with Ahasuerus, a wealthy king, giving an extravagant banquet, while Queen Vashti hosts a banquet for all the women in the palace. However, possibly out of a sense of virtue, she refuses to come before the king as he commanded. He became enraged, and "his anger burned within him" (Esther 1:12). He then banished Vashti for her disobedience and sent letters to all in the kingdom that "every man should be master in his own house" (1:22).

After having assembled a large number of attractive young virgins in his harem, he instructed each of them to receive twelve months of cosmetic treatments. From among these he chose Esther, "fair and beautiful" (2:7). The specifics of the king's idealized picture of beautiful women are not delineated in the text, but he clearly put great weight on appearances. Today there are specialists who have set standards for measuring the perfection of a woman's face that approximate *their* ideal of beauty. Male expectations and women's self-image—backed by constant messaging in the media—have generated whole industries of cosmetic surgery and makeup in an effort to remove or cover perceived imperfections. Some women may be attracted to a certain male physique, the more buff the better. Some men, noticing the inevitable signs of aging in their wives, such as wrinkles and graying hair, have opted to replace them with much younger trophy wives, as a way of enhancing their own prestige and becoming noticed in professional circles.

In Persia, the king becomes infatuated with Esther; however, unbeknown to him she is a Jew, the cousin of Mordecai. As queen, Esther uncovers a plot by Haman, the king's minister, to kill all the Jews. The king has Haman hung on a gallows meant for Mordecai. The Jews rejoice throughout the land. Today the Jews celebrate this victory over an archenemy on the feast of Purim.

Esther stands out as a woman who used her power in two notable ways: to bring justice to the wicked Haman and his henchmen, and as a consequence to play a key role in saving her people from destruction.

A Righteous Man and a Courageous Wife

Lament takes many forms. Recently, in Atlanta a man named Jeremy complained with this hand-written sign: "Not homeless—wife in Target 2+ hours," that he posted on Facebook to poke fun at the time she spends shopping. On a more serious note, UN Secretary-General António Guterres marked the 2021 International Women's Day by observing that during the COVID-19 pandemic there has been "a rollback in hard-won advances in women's rights" around the world. He asserted that "this is still a male-dominated world with a male-dominated culture."[61] An example is a recent study that ranks Afghanistan as one of the worst places to be a woman; in that country the illiteracy rate of women is 82 percent.

Is it good for a man or woman, a husband or wife, two partners, to challenge each other when there is a difference of perspective? What if the husband, considering himself to be a righteous man, dismisses his wife's challenge to what she may perceive as a narrow and suffocating religiosity? What if one partner in a relationship deals with major loss by saying: "This must have been God's will"? Perhaps you have had an experience like this or know someone who has. If so, you are in good company with Job and his wife.

Viewed from one perspective, Job and his wife remind us that in times of suffering the proper response to God may be that of lament. Protest may be more life-giving than silent acceptance, particularly when the suffering can be lessened—such as for the men, women, and children bearing the burden of famine and the ecological crisis resulting in a lack of clean water and air and increased global temperatures and water levels.

The Book of Job is a sustained debate by men about suffering. God allows Job, a righteous man, to be severely afflicted by Satan. Inexplicably, God puts all that Job has in Satan's power. This sets off a torrent of losses. Job's servants and livestock are wiped out, his ten sons and daughters are killed when the house they were in came crashing down upon them, and Job himself is afflicted with loathsome sores. With a potsherd to scrape his deteriorating flesh, Job is reduced to sitting among the ashes. What does God's agreement to have Job's integrity tested so severely say about God's own integrity?[62] Was the divine playing fair with a human who had trusted in God? The text begs the question.

A long and tiresome debate ensues. Job's so-called friends do their best to defend God's justice and the traditional theology of retribution—evil comes upon those who do evil—by trying to convince Job that he must have sinned to bring such misfortune upon himself. In his laments, Job protests his innocence. Finally, God speaks out of the whirlwind, but his message does not erase the mystery of suffering that overwhelmed this blameless man. Through a long litany of rhetorical questions, God points out Job's limited comprehension of divine power and God's sovereignty over all creation. Job responds by seemingly recognizing these limitations. In the epilogue, God restores what Job lost.

The Protests of Mrs. Job

Often overlooked in this wisdom book is the one salient reply by Job's unnamed wife to her dejected partner. Having suffered the loss of their livelihood and all their children, and with her husband infirm, she challenges him with the audacious question, "Do you still persist in your integrity?" and then commands this God-fearing man to do the unthinkable: "Curse God, and die." Does God care at all about her plight and the loss of her family? Job summarily dismisses her with the degrading retort: "You speak as any foolish woman would speak" (Job 2:9–10). Who today would not hear this as an insult to her sex? Jesus levies a harsh penalty for saying to another, "You fool": "you will be liable to the hell of fire" (Matthew 5:22). Though Job goes on to correctly, although sanctimoniously, point out that we should accept the bad from God as well as the good, the narrator seems to have doubled down on the patriarchal view of men's superior reasoning by setting up the only woman in the story as the foolish, doubting foil to wise, faithful Job.

If his wife can be called foolish for such an outburst, what about Job when he curses the day when he was born as well as God's role in it (3:3–4)? In his mood of darkness and gloom, he comes very close to doing what his wife had commanded. Job continues by casting aspersions on the day "because it did not shut the doors of my mother's womb," and regrets that there were "breasts for me to suck" (3:10, 12). In doing so, he denigrates his mother's womb and her breasts, implying that her body is the reason he lived to see these misfortunes. She's to blame; there is no mention of his father. What a contrast between Job's disparagement of the womb that bore him and Rachel's plea to Jacob: "Give me children, or I shall die!" Jacob replies that God is the one who withheld from her "the fruit of the womb" (Genesis 30:1–2).

The narrator says nothing about the grief of Job's wife, nor the anger she must have felt. This is the only time she speaks in all forty-two chapters. Her voice is silenced, and she is conspicuously absent in the epilogue, despite the detail of Job's restored fortunes (42:10–17). At one point Job laments that his wife is repulsed by him, and that "all my intimate friends abhor me, / and those whom I love have turned against me," probably also having his wife in mind (19:17, 19). Nonetheless, Job seems to have paid attention to her, for throughout his speeches he complains about and protests vigorously against God, an action God seems to approve of (42:7). Ultimately God stands in solidarity with Job. Then, at the end of the book, perhaps a later addition, Job divides his inheritance among his sons and daughters (42:15), a change in the right direction from patriarchal practices.

An Unlikely Marriage

Hosea was an eighth-century prophet from the northern kingdom of Israel who prophesied in an especially turbulent period: just before the destruction of Israel in 722 BC by the Assyrians. His oracles are best known for the marriage metaphor he uses to compare Israel's covenant with the Lord to a marriage between an unfaithful wife (Israel) and her husband (the Lord) who punishes and corrects her. Hosea accuses Israel of chasing after Canaanite lovers, in other words, worshipping their deities. Such worship may have included sexual rites. Incomprehensibly to our sensibilities, the Lord instructs the prophet to take a "wife of whoredom" and to have "children of whoredom" (1:2). Hosea's married life, then, mirrored Israel's relationship with the Lord. Like God, Hosea punishes his unfaithful wife, Gomer. After a period of time, the Lord commands Hosea to take her back.

Cheating that occurs in marriages can be absolutely devastating. The offended party often faces the agonizing choice of pursuing a divorce or seeking reconciliation. In the Gospel of Mark Jesus opposes all divorce (Mark 10:2–12), but in Matthew Jesus allows for an exception: "whoever divorces his wife, except for *porneia* (Greek, "unfaithfulness"), and marries another commits adultery" (Matthew 19:9). In the Catholic Church, which does not grant divorces, a divorced spouse can seek an annulment—a declaration, after careful examination, that the marriage was never valid in the first place—in order to be free to remarry in the Church. Such a course of action may be a time of grace and healing for some, and a painful process for others.

Returning to Hosea and his predicament, we recall that generally in ancient Israel marital relationships were socially male dominant, with wives subject to husbands. It would be a distortion to push the marriage metaphor so far that it portrays a male God punishing female Israel, the sinful one to the extent she is no longer redeemable. Rather, Hosea constructs the comparison to demonstrate God's compassion. We may wonder whether Gomer was really Hosea's wife or merely a character in his imagination. The details Hosea offers suggest the former. Her father and three children are named (1:3–9). She pursues lovers other than Hosea, yet he pursues her, to draw her back. To Hosea she is redeemable, just as Israel is in God's eyes.

What's a Mother to Do When Children Are Hungry?

Gomer was already a prostitute when the Lord instructed Hosea to marry her. Prostitution was the lot of many women of the ancient world, the vast majority of whom were forced into it for survival. Today, economic factors, including trafficking, account for the more than 40 million prostitutes in our world, of whom 80 percent are female and ranging in age between 13–25. Naming it a "sickness of humanity," Pope Francis called any form of prostitution "a reduction to slavery, a criminal act, a disgusting vice that confuses making love with venting out one's instincts by torturing a defenseless woman."[63]

Perhaps Gomer was such a woman who had found her only means of survival in selling her body. To be widowed at an early age, to be unwanted in marriage for whatever physical or mental reason and hence undesirable for subsequent marriages, or to be without working sons or an extended family were situations that effectively left an ancient woman few options besides prostitution.

Each child who resulted and who needed food and clothing exacerbated, even solidified, the woman's economic dependence on prostitution. Hosea may have told only one part of Gomer's story, what her prostitution symbolized to him. And that was indeed a profoundly prophetic message for Israel. The part that remains untold is that she was probably desperate on many levels, as are some women and men today, facing poverty, and perhaps apprehensive about giving up prostitution even after she married Hosea.

A Ranking Military Man and a Skeptical Apostle from Jerusalem

Cornelius was a Roman centurion of the Italian Cohort who lived in the important seaport of Caesarea. His story is told by Luke in Acts chapter 10. Cornelius, as his title indicates, would have commanded one hundred men, all of whom had to be Roman citizens to be in his cohort. Cornelius was a person of status with authority. Even as a Gentile, he "feared God with all his household; . . . gave alms generously . . . and prayed constantly" (10:2), a description which suggests he was actually a godfearer, a person closely attached to Judaism and possibly preparing to become fully Jewish. Full conversion, however, required circumcision for men, and many adult males opted not to do that (given the dangers of that type of ancient surgery for adults). They could still be attached to the Jewish community observing its dietary regulations and other laws, but they would have felt themselves to be more or less outsiders.

One afternoon Cornelius has a vision in which an angel tells him to send for Simon Peter who was staying in the nearby village of Joppa. Meanwhile Peter himself, while praying, falls into a trance in which he sees "the heaven opened and something like a large sheet coming down, being lowered to the ground by its four corners." In the sheet were "all kinds of four-footed creatures and reptiles and birds" (10:11–12). A voice tells Peter to kill and eat, but he refuses, since he had never before eaten unclean animals. The voice then told him, "What God has made clean, you must not call profane" (10:15). After this admonition is repeated three times, the sheet and animals are taken up to heaven. As Peter is puzzling over this vision, the men sent by Cornelius arrive, and Peter agrees to go to Caesarea with them the following day.

Although Peter knew that as a Jew he could not visit the home of a Gentile, he realized that in his vision God had shown him he "should not call anyone profane or unclean" (10:28). So he enters the house and teaches Cornelius and all those gathered there. When Peter then observes that the Holy Spirit is being poured out on Cornelius and the others, he orders them to be baptized. Peter thus opens the way for other Gentiles to join the Christ believers, although he probably had no idea that day how wide a door he opened. Initially many Gentile Christians felt like outsiders within the Jewish Christian movement, and it caused some disagreement. How ironic that over the centuries Gentile believers gradually outnumbered Jewish Christians. There is clearly a fluidity to the status of men and women: movement can take place from being outsiders to insiders.

A Businesswoman Offers Hospitality to the Apostle from Tarsus

Even though Philippi was a leading city of Macedonia, the Jews of that place were too small in number to have a synagogue building. Instead, they met outside the city on a riverbank. That is where Paul, in his quest to join other Jews for prayer, encounters a small community on a Sabbath day. He speaks to the women who were there, including Lydia. Luke offers a few details about her (Acts 16:14–15). She is a "worshiper of God," hence a Jewish sympathizer, perhaps meaning she was a godfearer in process of converting fully to Judaism. Luke also explains that she was originally from Thyatira (a city in the province of Lydia in Asia Minor) and that she dealt in purple cloth. That she is named for a province has prompted some to conclude that Lydia had been a slave and may have gained her freedom either by marriage or her work.

After hearing Paul's words, Lydia believed, and she along with the members of her household were baptized. Luke's comments suggest that since she herself was head of her household, she was at that time unmarried. Also, her occupation dealing in purple cloth was one which required some capital, namely to purchase the expensive purple dye as well as the cloth. Did she do the dyeing herself or was she a salesperson? Luke is not specific about where Lydia fit into the production and merchandising cycle, but his mention of her occupation does suggest she was economically well off, or at least stable. After her baptism Lydia quickly offers hospitality in her house to Paul and his coworker Silas. They must have accepted her invitation, since later in the narrative Luke notes that upon their subsequent arrest and release from prison they went to Lydia's house "and encouraged the brothers and sisters there" (Acts 16:40).

It is not insignificant that Lydia invites Paul with this condition: "If you have judged me to be faithful to the Lord, come and stay at my home" (16:15). Since Lydia was a Gentile, this reads like a challenge to Paul to "put your money where your mouth is!" If she was merely sympathetic to Judaism or in the process of becoming a Jewish convert, she was probably tired of being a second-class citizen among the Jews themselves, as "just a convert." It appears that Paul lived up to this challenge.

The Spirit Inspires Whomever the Spirit Wills

As Gentiles, Lydia and Cornelius represent those who had been drawn to the Jewish God and the profound teachings of Judaism. They were probably godfearers in the process of learning more about the traditions and laws. Whether they planned to fully convert or not, they would have known that socially they would always be seen in some way as outliers, not quite as Jewish as those born into the Jewish people. As welcomed as they may have been, they probably had a lingering sense of being on the periphery.

Christianity, by rapidly including godfearers and increasing numbers of non-Jewish believers into the Way (see Acts 9:2, 24:14) over the next few decades, offered a welcoming spiritual community with a new network of social connections. All believers were included under a big tent where there is room for everyone, as indicated in the message that Peter had received in his vision of the sheet with its motley assortment of all kinds of creatures. The author of Hebrews speaks about this extraordinary diversity of members as "so great a cloud of witnesses" (12:1).

For Reflection:

- Reflect on times in your life when you felt like an outsider. How did you respond? Who was there to extend a welcome?
- How might the grace of God be evident in men and women who feel like outliers from the faith community or society at large?

Afterword

Beyond the four Gospels in the New Testament, there is the ever unfolding fifth gospel—an expression used in multiple contexts—manifest in the lives of faithful women and men who chart the course of their vocations in response to the call of the Holy One. Seeking neither human perfection nor divine exaltation, they are living icons of the Creator—even in their fallible choices, their manifold disappointments, and their bruised relationships.

We have striven in this book to outline the main characteristics of the complex issues involved in the identity of women and men. We have seen that the Bible shows the great diversity that exists in humanity, and that the interrelationship between women and men is not always easy to comprehend. We encountered characters of both sexes who had both good and bad characteristics. We also saw that, from a faith perspective, all humans are to reflect the ideal of their Creator. We are beautifully made and are called to reflect this beauty by the way we live in the world with our sisters and brothers, who equally reflect this goodness.

We acknowledge that we have not been able to explore every issue tied to this topic, even less to resolve some of the complexities that have become more evident in the modern era. Nevertheless, our own experience as a married couple and as biblical scholars has led us to a greater appreciation of how we are called to mirror the goodness of our

Creator. If it is true, as the psalmist writes, that all of us have been made “a little lower than God,” and that we have been crowned “with glory and honor” (Psalm 8:5), might it be possible to embrace this profound dignity in ourselves even when we struggle with the barnacles that have become encrusted on our better selves? Even more, what might it be like if we were regularly mindful to approach one another with the awareness that we are all among the mortals for whom God cares (Psalm 8:4), that all have their place in close company with the Creator?

Notes

1. https://www.washingtonpost.com/dc-md-va/2021/06/22/first-population-estimate-lgbtq-non-binary-adults-us-is-out-heres-why-that-matters/.
2. Pope Benedict XVI, General Audience, "Women at the service of the Gospel," February 14, 2007, https://www.vatican.va/content/benedict-xvi/en/audiences/2007/documents/hf_ben-xvi_aud_20070214.html.
3. "The Gospel of the Marginalized Is Where Our Credibility Is Found and Revealed" http://www.educatio.va/content/dam/cec/Documenti/19_0997_INGLESE.pdf.
4. Michael G. Lawler and Todd A. Salzman, "The Catholic Church must listen to transgender and intersex people" (2020). https://www.ncronline.org/news/opinion/catholic-church-must-listen-transgender-and-intersex-people.
5. Paragraph 19. http://www.educatio.va/content/dam/cec/Documenti/19_0997_INGLESE.pdf.
6. https://www.genome.gov/about-genomics/fact-sheets/Genetics-vs-Genomics.
7. "'The American Dream,' Sermon Delivered at Ebenezer Baptist Church." https://kinginstitute.stanford.edu/king-papers/documents/american-dream-sermon-delivered-ebenezer-baptist-church.
8. *Fratelli Tutti*, paragraphs 23, 121.
9. *Fratelli Tutti*, paragraph 24.
10. https://godinallthings.com/2021/01/11/the-neighbourhood/.
11. *The Woman's Bible* (Global Grey ebooks, 2018), 25-26.
12. See respectively the Global Gender Gap Report 2021 and the U.S. Bureau of Statistics for 2020.
13. https://www.ncronline.org/blogs/young-voices/beyond-churchs-wage-gap.

14. https://www.washingtonpost.com/news/acts-of-faith/wp/2015/04/29/pope-francis-its-pure-scandal-that-women-earn-less-than-men-for-the-same-work/.
15. https://hbr.org/2019/06/research-women-score-higher-than-men-in-most-leadership-skills.
16. "On the Question of Admission of Women to the Ministerial Priesthood" (October 15, 1976), section 6; http://www.vatican.va/roman_curia/congregations/cfaith/documents/rc_con_cfaith_doc_19761015_inter-insigniores_en.html.
17. Florence Gillman, *Women Who Knew Paul* (Collegeville, MN: Liturgical Press, 1992).
18. See Aidan Kavanagh, *The Shape of Baptism: The Rite of Christian Initiation* (Collegeville, MN: Liturgical Press, 1978).
19. See Pope Paul VI's Apostolic Exhortation, *Marialis Cultus* (1974).
20. https://ronrolheiser.com/the-mary-of-scripture-and-the-mary-of-devotions/#.YGtELOhKjcc.
21. https://angelusnews.com/faith/once-again-pope-francis-says-mary-is-not-the-co-redemptrix/.
22. https://www.ncbi.nlm.nih.gov/pmc/articles/PMC5022769/.
23. https://www.americamagazine.org/faith/2019/01/11/how-catholic-church-can-help-single-mothers.
24. Warren Carter, "Joseph," *New Interpreters Dictionary of the Bible*, vol. 3 (Nashville: Abingdon, 2008), 402.
25. "Mary of Nazareth: Friend of God and Prophet," *America Magazine* (June 17, 2000). https://www.americamagazine.org/faith/2000/06/17/mary-nazareth-friend-god-and-prophet.
26. https://www.nytimes.com/2020/11/27/us/border-mexico-pregnant-women.html.
27. *Luke*, Wisdom Commentary, vol. 43 (Collegeville, MN: Liturgical Press, 2021), 17.
28. John P. Meier, "The Brothers and Sisters of Jesus in Ecumenical Perspective," *Catholic Biblical Quarterly* 54 (1992): 1-28, here 26.

29. See Susanna Asikainen, "Women out of Place: The Women Who Challenged Jesus," *Neotestamentica* 52:1 (2018): 179-193, here 186.

30. https://ronrolheiser.com/joseph-and-christmas/#.YG3pyuhKjcc.

31. For much of the following, we rely on Susan E. Haddox, "Is There a 'Biblical Masculinity'? Masculinities in the Hebrew Bible," *Word & World* 36:1 (2016) 5-14.

32. Haddox, "Biblical Masculinity," 8.

33. Haddox, "Biblical Masculinity," 8.

34. Frederick Buechner, *The Magnificent Defeat*. Frederick Buechner, ed. (New York: HarperOne, 1985), 15. Quoted by John Peterson, "Wrestling with 'Half-Gods': Biblical Discourse in Mary Austin's *The Ford*," *Christianity & Literature* 6714 (2018), 653-668, p. 659.

35. https://www.romereports.com/en/2020/06/10/pope-reflects-on-jacob-wrestling-with-the-angel-prayer-is-not-always-easy/.

36. Susan E. Haddox, "Masculinity Studies of the Hebrew Bible: The First Two Decades," *Currents in Biblical Research* 14.2 (2016) 176-206, 186.

37. Haddox, "Masculinity Studies," 189.

38. Haddox, "Masculinity Studies," 191.

39. See Armin M. Kummer, *Men, Spirituality, and Gender-specific Biblical Hermeneutics* (Leuven: Peeters, 2019), 109-114.

40. See *Give Us This Day*. May Issue (Collegeville, MN: Liturgical Press, 2021), 155.

41. *Dante. The Divine Comedy,* translated by Mark Musa (New York: Penguin Classics, 1984).

42. See Alice L. Laffey and Mahri Leonard-Fleckman, *Ruth*. Wisdom Commentary 8 (Collegeville, MN: Liturgical Press, 2017), 14-15.

43. Gale A. Yee, "Ruth," in *Fortress Commentary on the Bible. The Old Testament and Apocrypha*, edited by Gale A. Yee, Hugh R. Page Jr., and Matthew J. M. Doober (Minneapolis, MN: Fortress, 214), 353.

44. Yee, "Ruth," 359.

45. See Florence M. Gillman, "Bernice at Paul's Witness to the Resurrection," in *Resurrection in the New Testament. Festchrift J. Lambrecht. Bibliotheca Ephemeridum Theologicarum Lovaniensium* CLXV (Leuven, Peeters: 2002), 249-264.
46. *This Tremendous Lover* (Gastonia, NC: Thomas More Press, 1963, originally 1946).
47. https://www.vatican.va/content/francesco/en/motu_proprio/documents/papa-francesco-motu-proprio-20210510_antiquum-ministerium.html.
48. https://www.vatican.va/content/john-paul-ii/en/messages/peace/documents/hf_jp-ii_mes_08121994_xxviii-world-day-for-peace.html.
49. https://www.catholicnewsagency.com/news/36050/pope-points-to-mary-magdalene-as-an-apostle-of-hope.
50. Dorothy A. Lee, *The Ministry of Women in the New Testament* (Grand Rapids, MI: Baker Academic, 2021), 53.
51. Lee, *Ministry of Women*, 52.
52. See Reid, Matthews, *Luke*, vol. 43B (2021), 355.
53. Lee, *Women in Ministry*, 91.
54. See Asikainen, "Women out of Place," 182-184.
55. Jennifer Larson, "Paul's Masculinity," *Journal of Biblical Literature* 123:1 (2004) 85-97, here 94.
56. https://www.vatican.va/content/francesco/en/audiences/2019/documents/papa-francesco_20191113_udienza-generale.html; accessed August 6, 2021.
57. https://www.theguardian.com/world/2021/mar/09/shoot-me-instead-myanmar-nuns-plea-to-spare-protesters; accessed April 20, 2021.
58. https://www.catholicnewsagency.com/news/247258/cardinal-bo-we-need-the-light-of-gods-mercy-in-myanmar; accessed April 20, 2021.
59. https://www.americamagazine.org/faith/2019/01/11/how-catholic-church-can-help-single-mothers.

60. https://www.americamagazine.org/faith/2021/04/22/women-bibile-infertility-scripture-240494; accessed April 23, 2021.

61. https://abcnews.go.com/US/wireStory/international-womens-day-laments-retreat-rights-76334124.

62. See Jonathan Kangwa, "Woman and Nature in the Book of Job: An African Eco-Feminist Reading," *Feminist Theology* 29:1 (2020) 75-90, here 78.

63. https://www.americamagazine.org/faith/2019/07/30/pope-francis-prostitution-sickness-humanity.

New City Press is one of more than 20 publishing houses sponsored by the Focolare, a movement founded by Chiara Lubich to help bring about the realization of Jesus' prayer: "That all may be one" (John 17:21). In view of that goal, New City Press publishes books and resources that enrich the lives of people and help all to strive toward the unity of the entire human family. We are a member of the Association of Catholic Publishers.

www.newcitypress.com
202 Comforter Blvd.
Hyde Park, New York

Periodicals
Living City Magazine
www.livingcitymagazine.com

Scan to join our mailing list
for discounts and promotions
or go to www.newcitypress.com
and click on "join our email list."